THE AUDACITY TO BELIEVE THAT I AM FREE

BY

I0360190

BRUCE E. FORD

HOW TO MAXIMIZE YOUR FULL POTENTIAL DESPITE YOUR ENVIRONMENT

Life Is A Journey...

EMBRYORGANIC MULTI-MEDIA

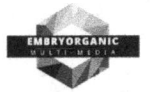

THE BOOK...

Published by Krystal Lee Enterprises (KLE Publishing)
Copyright © 2025 by Bruce Ford All rights reserved.
Please send comments and questions:

Krystal Lee Enterprises
770-240-0089 Ext. 1
sales@KLEPub.com

To Reach the Author:
Email: bookbruceford@gmail.com

Social Media: @bookbruceford @brucefordspeaks

Printed in the United States of America.
All rights reserved. No part of this book may be reproduced or transmitted in any form or by any means, electronic or mechanical, including photocopying, recording or any information storage and retrieval system without written permission of the publisher except for brief quotations used in reviews, written specifically for inclusion in a newspaper, blog, magazine, or academic paper.

ISBN: 978-1-945066-93-1

The Audacity To Believe I Am Free

Dedication

To my parents, Mr. and Mrs. JD Ford, Thank you for the sacrifices that you made for me and my two older brothers. Your unwavering support and love have been the cornerstone of my journey to freedom. To my ancestors and current family members, young and old, I carry your legacy with pride and gratitude. Your resilience and strength continue to inspire me to believe in the audacity of freedom.

To the teachers who nurtured my mind and the neighborhood friends who shared in my adventures, especially Anthony Johnson, Your guidance and camaraderie have left an indelible mark on my heart and my pursuit of liberty. To my best friend and cousin, Allan Ford, Your companionship has been a constant source of courage and determination on this path to freedom. To my son, Austin Ford, You are my eternal source of inspiration. Your existence propels me to strive for a world where the audacity to believe in freedom is a reality for all. To my beautiful niece, Olivia H. Ford, Your generous and beautiful heart encouraged me to prevail, and for that, I am eternally grateful. This book is dedicated to my family, for you are the embodiment of the audacity to believe that we are free.

Contents

Preface	I
Introduction	Iv
1. Have A Good Understanding	1
2. Becoming So Superior and Knowledgable	15
3. Don't Get Caught In Other People Stuff	27
4. Ethnic Repression and Unfairness	37
5. Excellence	42
6. Internal Area: The Ultimate Frontier	55
7. Utilize or Suffer Defeat	69
8. Catch the Attention of Like Minded People	88
9. Tranquilty of the Mind - Freedom from all Negative Emotions	102
10. Devoted Emotions - Do Unto Others	115

Preface

In the realm of human existence, the audacity to believe is a powerful force. It is the beacon that guides us through the darkest storms and propels us toward the brightest horizons. It is the unwavering faith that resides deep within our hearts, reminding us that we are, indeed, free to shape our destinies and transcend the limitations that surround us.

Welcome to "The Audacity to Believe I Am Free." This book is a voyage through the profound principles that have breathed life into the soul of the author, Bruce E. Ford, and fueled his inexhaustible motivation. In the following pages, you will embark on a journey of self-discovery and empowerment, as we dissect the ten guiding stars that have illuminated Bruce's path to purpose and prosperity.

Chapter by chapter, we delve into the wisdom encapsulated within each title, uncovering the secrets to a life defined by purpose, success, and unwavering belief. These principles are not mere theories; they are the bedrock upon which Bruce has built a life of meaning, abundance, and boundless possibility.

"Have Good Understanding" explores the profound impact of knowledge and the importance of deepening our understanding of the world around us. "Becoming So Superior, So Knowledgeable" challenges us to rise above mediocrity and strive for excellence in all that we do. "Don't Get Caught in Other People's Stuff!" reminds us to guard our energy and focus on our own path, free from the distractions of negativity.

The Audacity To Believe I Am Free

We confront the weight of "Ethnic Repression and Unfairness" and emerge stronger, understanding that adversity can be a catalyst for transformation. "Excellence" becomes our mantra as we embark on a quest for self-improvement, knowing that the pursuit of greatness is the highest calling.

Our inner world is explored in "Internal Area: The Ultimate Frontier," where we unlock the power of self-awareness and mindfulness. "Utilize or Suffer Defeat" teaches us that our choices determine our destiny, urging us to harness the power of our decisions.

"Catch the Attention of Like-Minded People" reveals the importance of building a supportive community and the strength that comes from shared visions. In the tranquility of "Tranquility of the Mind - Freedom from All Negative Emotions," we find the key to emotional freedom and lasting peace.

"Devoted Relations - Do Unto Others" emphasizes the significance of compassion and reciprocity in our interactions with others. "Commendable Goals and Principles" shows us the path to true happiness lies in pursuing virtuous goals.

"Prosperity Is Your Right!" reaffirms our entitlement to a life of abundance and success. "Your Thoughts Are the Lone Thing You Dictate" is a poignant reminder that we are the masters of our thoughts, and they shape our reality.

"Thoughts: Dreams in Battle" teaches us to guard our dreams fiercely and protect them from the storms of doubt. "From Bondage to Treasures" is a testament to the resilience of the human spirit in the face of adversity.

Finally, we unlock the boundless wellspring of creativity within us in "Unlocking Your Innate Creativeness," embracing the limitless potential that resides in our imagination.

As you journey through these pages, let the words of Bruce E. Ford be your guiding light. Let his experiences, wisdom, and unwavering belief in the audacity to believe inspire you to take bold steps toward your dreams, to embrace your freedom, and to live a life that is truly your own.

"The Audacity to Believe I Am Free" is not just a book; it is a blueprint for transformation. It is an invitation to unlock the extraordinary potential that resides within you. So, dear reader, let us embark on this remarkable journey together and discover the audacity to believe in our own freedom.

May these pages be a source of inspiration, empowerment, and the audacity to believe. Welcome aboard.

Introduction

In a world brimming with narratives and experiences, the concept of freedom holds an exalted place. It is a word with boundless meanings, one that evokes sentiments of hope, longing, and perseverance. Freedom is the siren's call of the human spirit, beckoning us to pursue it with an audacious belief that it can be attained.

"The Audacity To Believe I Am Free" is a chronicle of this extraordinary journey, an exploration of the profound and often deeply personal moments in the lives of those who dared to dream of freedom. This book invites you to join us on a voyage through time and space, guided by the shared experiences of individuals who have faced adversity and injustice, yet refused to surrender to despair.

Here, we delve into the stories of those who have drawn strength from their families and ancestors, who have been inspired by the wisdom of teachers and the camaraderie of friends. We also encounter the unwavering support of loved ones and the enduring bonds of friendship, as well as the profound influence of a child who becomes the driving force behind an unyielding quest for liberation.

This narrative is a tapestry of diverse voices, backgrounds, and aspirations, all woven together by the common thread of belief. Belief in the possibility of freedom, in the audacity to defy circumstances and expectations, and in the resilience of the human spirit. As we explore these stories, we aim to inspire you, the reader, to reflect upon your own journey and to nurture the audacity to believe in your own freedom, whatever form it may take.

The Audacity To Believe I Am Free

Throughout the pages of this book, we will confront challenges, witness triumphs, and ultimately, embrace the power of the human spirit to defy all odds. We will confront the paradox that freedom is both an individual and collective pursuit, intertwined with the destinies of families, communities, and societies.

"The Audacity To Believe I Am Free" is a testament to the enduring human spirit, an affirmation that even in the face of the most formidable obstacles, we have the capacity to believe, to strive, and to achieve the freedom we yearn for. It is an invitation to join us on a transformative journey—a journey that explores the profound meaning of freedom and the audacity it takes to claim it as our own.

HAVE GOOD UNDERSTANDING

Chapter 1

Proverbs 3:13 (KJV)
"Happy is the man that findeth wisdom, and the man that getteth understanding."

Psalm 111:10 – The fear of the Lord is the beginning of wisdom; all who follow his precepts have good understanding. To him belongs eternal praise.

Psalm 110:11 states that the fear of the Lord is the beginning of wisdom, and those who follow his precepts gain good understanding. The psalm concludes by acknowledging God's eternal praise.

The fear of the Lord mentioned in Psalm 111:10 refers to a reverential awe and respect for God. This fear is not rooted in terror, but rather in a deep understanding of God's power and goodness. When we approach God with reverence, we open ourselves up to receiving wisdom and understanding from Him. Following God's precepts is another important aspect of gaining wisdom. His commandments and teachings are meant to guide us in living a fulfilling and purposeful life. The psalm's conclusion about God's eternal praise reminds us that God is worthy of our worship and adoration. As we seek to grow in wisdom and understanding, let us continue to acknowledge and praise the One who created and sustains us.

Approaching God with reverence and following His precepts are key aspects of gaining wisdom and living a fulfilling life. However, it is important to note that gaining wisdom is not a one-time achievement, but rather a lifelong pursuit. We must strive to continuously learn, grow, and apply God's teachings to our daily lives.

One way to gain wisdom is through prayer and meditation on God's word. By spending time in His presence and seeking His guidance, we can deepen our understanding of His will for our lives. Another important aspect of gaining wisdom is seeking counsel from others who are also seeking to live according to God's precepts. Surrounding ourselves with a community of believers who encourage and challenge us can help us to stay on the path of wisdom.

As we continue to seek wisdom and understanding, let us never forget to praise and worship the God who created and sustains us. Let us give Him the honor and adoration He deserves, both now and for all eternity.

It's essential to remember that the pursuit of wisdom is a lifelong journey, and we must continually seek to grow in our understanding of God's teachings. Here are some additional tips to help you gain wisdom and live a fulfilling life:

- Read the Bible regularly to gain a deeper understanding of God's word.
- Attend church services and participate in Bible studies to learn from others and build a community of believers.
- Practice gratitude and thanksgiving to develop a positive outlook on life and appreciate the blessings around you.
- Seek out opportunities to serve and help others, which can provide valuable lessons and insights into God's character.
- Practice discernment and seek wise counsel before making important decisions, to ensure that your actions align with God's will.

Ultimately, the pursuit of wisdom is about seeking a deeper relationship with God, and honoring Him with our thoughts, words, and actions. Let us continue to seek His guidance and give Him the praise and worship He deserves.

Proverbs 3:5–6 (NKJV)
"Trust in the Lord with all your heart,
And lean not on your own understanding;
In all your ways acknowledge Him,
And He shall direct your paths."

Summary:

Psalm 111:10 teaches that the fear of the Lord is the beginning of wisdom, and following His precepts leads to understanding. Seeking wisdom is a lifelong journey that involves approaching God with reverence, following His teachings, and surrounding ourselves with a community of believers. The pursuit of wisdom involves reading the Bible regularly, attending church, practicing gratitude, serving others, and seeking wise counsel. Ultimately, seeking wisdom is about deepening our relationship with God and giving Him the praise and worship He deserves.

Put GOD first and foremost.

It's so important to have faith and a sense of purpose in our lives. Prioritizing our relationship with a higher power can provide us with guidance, comfort, and strength during difficult times. Whether it's through prayer, meditation, or other spiritual practices, taking time to connect with something greater than ourselves can bring a sense of peace and perspective to our lives. It's wonderful that you recognize the value of this and are making it a priority. Keep up the good work!

Adding context to this, spirituality and faith have been important aspects of human culture for centuries. People across different religions and beliefs have found solace in connecting with a higher power. This practice isn't just about religion, but it's also about understanding ourselves and the world around us. It's about finding meaning and purpose in our lives, which can bring a sense of fulfillment that cannot be found elsewhere.

If you're new to spirituality or religion, it can be overwhelming to know where to start. But, taking small steps like incorporating mindfulness practices, attending religious services or joining a support group can be helpful. It's also important to remember that everyone's spiritual journey is unique, and what works for one person may not work for another.

Remember to be patient and compassionate with yourself as you navigate your spiritual journey. It takes time, effort, and dedication to build a meaningful connection with a higher power, but the rewards are immeasurable. Keep exploring and discovering what works for you, and you'll find the peace and guidance you seek.

Spirituality and faith are not only important for personal growth and development but also for mental and physical well-being. It has been found that individuals who practice spirituality experience lower levels of stress, anxiety, and depression. This is because spirituality provides a sense of purpose, meaning, and direction in life, which can help individuals cope with difficult situations.

If you're interested in exploring spirituality, there are many resources available to you. You can start by reading books or attending workshops and seminars that focus on different aspects of spirituality. You can also seek out a mentor or spiritual guide who can offer guidance and support as you embark on your journey.

It's important to note that spirituality is a personal experience and there's no one-size-fits-all approach. What works for one person may not work for another, so it's essential to be patient and compassionate with yourself as you explore different practices and beliefs. Remember that spirituality is a journey, not a destination, and there's always room for growth and discovery.

Philippians 1:6 (NIV)
"Being confident of this, that he who began a good work in you will carry it on to completion until the day of Christ Jesus."

Summary:

Prioritizing our relationship with a higher power can provide guidance, comfort, and strength during difficult times. Spirituality and faith have been important aspects of human culture for centuries, offering a sense of fulfillment that cannot be found elsewhere. Practicing spirituality has been linked to lower levels of stress, anxiety, and depression. Everyone's spiritual journey is unique, and it's important to be patient and compassionate with yourself as you explore different practices and beliefs.

Get hold of the wisdom and persistence to intelligently and effectively observe your situation

Acquire the insight and determination to thoughtfully and efficiently assess your circumstances. By taking the time to assess your circumstances, you can gain a better understanding of your current situation and identify any areas that may need improvement. Here are some ways you can acquire insight and determination to assess your circumstances thoughtfully and efficiently:

- *Practice mindfulness:* Take time each day to reflect on your thoughts and feelings. This can help you become more aware of your current circumstances and identify any patterns or habits that may be holding you back.

Proverbs 4:7 (NIV)
"The beginning of wisdom is this: Get wisdom.
Though it cost all you have, get understanding."

- *Seek feedback from others*: Ask trusted friends, family members, or colleagues for their perspective on your situation. They may be able to offer valuable insights or suggestions you haven't considered.
- *Set goals:* Identify specific, measurable goals that align with your desired outcomes. This can help you stay focused and motivated as you work to improve your circumstances.
- *Take action:* Once you have identified areas for improvement, take action to address them. This may involve making changes to your daily routine, seeking additional training or education, or seeking out new opportunities.

Assessing your circumstances is an ongoing process, and it's important to be patient and persistent as you work to achieve your goals. To further improve your circumstances, here are some additional suggestions that may be helpful:

- *Keep a journal*: Writing down your thoughts and experiences can help you gain clarity and perspective on your situation. You can also use your journal to track your progress, celebrate your successes, and identify areas where you still need to improve.
- *Get professional help:* If you're struggling with a specific issue, consider seeking the help of a professional, such as a therapist or coach. They can provide you with valuable guidance and support as you work to overcome challenges and achieve your goals.
- *Expand your network*: Building relationships with people who share your interests and goals can be a valuable source of support and inspiration. Attend networking events, join online groups, or take classes to meet new people and expand your circle.

- *Embrace change:* Sometimes, the only way to improve your circumstances is to make a big change. Be open to new opportunities and experiences, even if they seem scary or unfamiliar at first. Remember that growth often requires stepping outside of your comfort zone.

By incorporating these strategies into your life, you can gain a deeper understanding of your circumstances and take meaningful steps to improve them. Remember to stay focused, stay positive, and stay committed to your goals.
It's important to continuously work towards improving your circumstances. Here are a few more suggestions that may be helpful:

- *Practice gratitude:* Take time each day to reflect on the things you are grateful for. This can help shift your focus towards the positive aspects of your life and improve your overall mood.
- *Learn a new skill*: Expanding your knowledge and skillset can open up new opportunities and help you feel more confident in your abilities. Consider taking a class or workshop in something that interests you.

- *Take care of your physical health:* Your physical well-being can have a significant impact on your overall happiness and success. Make sure you're getting enough sleep, eating a balanced diet, and engaging in regular exercise.
- *Set realistic goals:* It's important to have a clear idea of what you want to achieve and how you plan to get there. However, it's equally important to set goals that are achievable and realistic. Break your larger goals into smaller, more manageable steps to help you stay motivated and on track.

Summary:

Improving your circumstances takes time and effort, but the results can be well worth it. Stay focused, stay positive, and keep working towards your goals.

To improve your circumstances, it is important to assess your situation thoughtfully and efficiently. Practice mindfulness, seek feedback from others, set goals, and take action. Keeping a journal, getting professional help, expanding your network, and embracing change are additional ways to improve your circumstances. Additionally, practicing gratitude, learning a new skill, taking care of your physical health, and setting realistic goals can further help in achieving your desired outcomes.

Improvement takes time and effort, but the results are worth it.

There's nothing more disgraceful than the person who wastes his or her life traveling from one fixation to another

Constantly obsessing over new interests can be a waste of time and ultimately lead to a sense of shame or disappointment. It is important to note that having a variety of interests is not inherently bad. However, constantly jumping from one interest to another without fully exploring or committing to them can be unproductive. This behavior can also make it difficult to build mastery or expertise in any particular area. Additionally, the pressure to constantly discover new interests can stem from external societal pressures or a fear of missing out. It's important to take the time to reflect on what truly brings joy and fulfillment, rather than constantly seeking out new things to do or try. It's okay to take a break and stick with something for a while, even if it may not be the "hottest" or most popular interest at the moment.

The Audacity To Believe I Am Free

Expanding on the idea of exploring interests, it's worth noting that it's okay to not have everything figured out right away. Sometimes it takes trying different things to discover what truly resonates with us. This process of self-discovery can be exciting, but it can also be overwhelming. It's important to be patient with ourselves and to not compare our journey to others. Everyone has their own unique path, and what works for one person may not work for another.

In addition to taking the time to reflect on our interests, it's also important to consider how we spend our time. It's easy to get caught up in the hustle and bustle of daily life, but taking breaks to recharge and do things we enjoy can actually improve productivity and overall well-being. Finding a balance between exploring new interests and nurturing existing ones can help us lead more fulfilling lives.

One way to approach exploring our interests is by setting small goals for ourselves. These could be as simple as trying a new hobby for an hour a week or attending a workshop related to a topic we are curious about. By breaking down our interests into manageable tasks, we can avoid feeling overwhelmed and gain a sense of accomplishment along the way.

Another important aspect of self-discovery is being open to new experiences and perspectives. It's easy to fall into a routine and stick with what's comfortable, but stepping outside of our comfort zone can lead to new insights and personal growth. This could mean trying a new type of cuisine, traveling to a new place or meeting new people who have different backgrounds and beliefs.

Ultimately, the key to finding fulfillment in our lives is to prioritize the things that bring us joy and make us feel alive. Whether it's pursuing a passion project or simply taking a walk in nature, making time for the things that matter to us can have a positive impact on our well-being and overall quality of life.

Summary:

Constantly obsessing over new interests can be unproductive, leading to a sense of shame or disappointment. It's important to reflect on what brings joy and fulfillment, instead of constantly seeking out new things to do or try. Finding a balance between exploring new interests and nurturing existing ones can help lead to a fulfilling life. Setting small goals, being open to new experiences and perspectives, and prioritizing the things that bring joy can lead to personal growth and a positive impact on well-being.

Your start on the path to achievement can be found somewhere within your present environment

The first step towards achieving your goals can be found by looking at your current surroundings and circumstances. Building on this statement, it's important to note that taking stock of your current surroundings doesn't necessarily mean accepting them as they are. Rather, it can serve as a starting point for identifying areas where you can make changes and take action towards achieving your goals. Here are some additional thoughts to consider:

- Reflect on what aspects of your current surroundings are helping or hindering your progress towards your goals.
- Consider how you can leverage your strengths and resources to overcome any obstacles that may be standing in your way.
- Don't be afraid to seek out new opportunities and experiences that can help you move closer to your goals.
- Remember that achieving your goals is a process, and it may require adjustments and course corrections along the way. The key is to stay focused and committed to your vision.

The Audacity To Believe I Am Free

Expanding on the topic of achieving your goals by taking stock of your current surroundings, it's important to recognize that this process can be a catalyst for positive change. Here are some additional ideas to consider:

- Once you have identified areas where you can make changes, create an action plan with specific steps you can take to move closer to your goals. This can help you stay focused and motivated.
- It's important to be honest with yourself about what is and isn't working in your current situation. This can be a difficult but necessary step towards making meaningful progress.
- Surround yourself with people who support and encourage you. Seek out mentors or peers who can provide guidance and accountability as you work towards your goals.
- Be patient and kind to yourself throughout the process. Remember that setbacks and challenges are a natural part of any journey. Celebrate your successes, no matter how small they may seem.

By taking a proactive approach to your current surroundings and using them as a launching point for personal growth, you can make meaningful progress towards achieving your goals. Continuing on the topic of achieving one's goals, it's important to recognize that the process of taking stock of your current surroundings can also help you gain a better understanding of your values and priorities. By reflecting on what is and isn't working in your life, you can identify areas where you may need to make changes in order to align your actions with your goals.

In addition to creating an action plan and seeking out support from others, it's also important to cultivate a growth mindset. This means approaching challenges as opportunities for learning and growth, rather than as obstacles to be avoided or feared. By reframing setbacks as opportunities to learn and improve, you can stay motivated and focused on your goals.

Ultimately, the journey towards achieving your goals is a personal one, and it's important to stay true to yourself and your values along the way. By taking a proactive approach to your current surroundings and using them as a launching point for personal growth, you can make meaningful progress towards achieving your goals and living a fulfilling life.

Summary:

To achieve your goals, start by looking at your current surroundings.
Identify what is helping and hindering your progress, leverage strengths and resources, and seek out new opportunities. Create an action plan, be honest with yourself, surround yourself with supporters, and be patient. Taking stock of your current surroundings can help gain a better understanding of your values and priorities. Cultivate a growth mindset, reframe setbacks as opportunities, and stay true to yourself and your values.

Preparation is the key

The importance of being prepared in order to achieve success or avoid problems. Being prepared is a key factor in achieving success or avoiding problems in any aspect of life. Here are some additional thoughts on the importance of being prepared:

- Being prepared helps you to anticipate potential problems and develop solutions before they occur.
- It allows you to make informed decisions and take calculated risks, rather than making hasty or uninformed choices.
- Being prepared can also boost your confidence, as you feel more capable and in control of the situation.
- It can help you to save time and resources in the long run, as you have already taken the necessary steps to be ready for whatever may come your way.

Overall, being prepared is an essential component of achieving success and avoiding problems. By investing the time and effort to prepare yourself, you can increase your chances of success and minimize the negative impact of any challenges that may arise. Here are some additional points to consider regarding the importance of being prepared:

- Being prepared allows you to adapt to unexpected situations quickly. When you have a plan in place, you are able to adjust your actions and pivot when necessary, rather than being caught off guard.
- It also helps you to prioritize your goals and stay focused on what's important. By taking the time to prepare, you can identify what steps are necessary to achieve your objectives and make progress towards them.
- Being prepared can also improve your communication skills. When you have a clear plan and know what you want to achieve, it's easier to articulate your goals to others and collaborate effectively.
- Lastly, being prepared can help you to build resilience. When you encounter setbacks or obstacles, you are better equipped to bounce back and keep moving forward.

Being prepared is not just about avoiding problems, but also about creating opportunities for success. It's an ongoing process that requires effort and dedication, but the benefits are well worth it. It's important to note that being prepared is not only beneficial in our personal lives but also in the workplace. Here are some additional ways in which being prepared can have a positive impact on your career:

Proverbs 21:5 (NIV)
"The plans of the diligent lead to profit
as surely as haste leads to poverty."

- It can help you to stand out as a proactive and reliable employee. Employers appreciate individuals who take the initiative to plan ahead and anticipate potential challenges.
- Being prepared can also increase your confidence and reduce stress levels. When you feel prepared for a meeting or presentation, for example, you're more likely to feel calm and collected, which can help you to perform better.
- It can lead to better time management and increased productivity. By having a plan in place, you're able to make the most of your time and avoid wasting it on unimportant tasks.
- Lastly, being prepared can improve your problem-solving skills. When you're used to thinking ahead and considering different scenarios, you're more likely to come up with creative solutions when faced with a challenging situation.

In short, being prepared is a valuable skill that can benefit us in many different areas of our lives. By taking the time to plan and prepare, we can increase our chances of success and become more resilient in the face of adversity.

Summary:

Being prepared is essential for achieving success and avoiding problems. It helps to anticipate potential problems, make informed decisions, boost confidence, save time and resources, adapt to unexpected situations, prioritize goals, improve communication skills, and build resilience. Being prepared is not only beneficial in our personal lives, but also in the workplace as it can lead to better time management, increased productivity, and improved problem-solving skills. Overall, being prepared is a valuable skill that can benefit us in many different areas of our lives.

BECOMING SO SUPERIOR, SO KNOWLEDGEABLE

Chapter 2

1 Corinthians 8:1 (NIV)
"We know that 'We all possess knowledge.' But knowledge puffs up while love builds up."

It means becoming so superior, so knowledgeable at what you're doing that you actually force the break you seek to come your way

The phrase suggests that by mastering your craft and becoming an expert, you can create opportunities for yourself and achieve your goals. Becoming an expert in your field can indeed open doors to opportunities that may not have been available otherwise. Here are some ways in which mastering your craft can help you achieve your goals:

- *Recognition:* When you become an expert, people start to take notice of your work and recognize your skills. This can lead to more opportunities, such as speaking engagements, collaborations, and job offers.
- *Credibility:* Being an expert in your field gives you credibility, which can be invaluable when it comes to pitching ideas, products, or services. People are more likely to trust and invest in someone who has a track record of success.
- *Innovation:* When you know your craft inside and out, you are better equipped to innovate and come up with new ideas. This can lead to breakthroughs in your industry and give you a competitive edge.

Overall, mastering your craft takes time and effort, but it can be well worth it in the long run. By becoming an expert, you can create opportunities for yourself, achieve your goals, and make a real impact in your field.

Mastering your craft is essential for anyone who wants to be successful in their field. It is a continuous process that requires dedication, hard work, and a willingness to learn. Here are some additional points that can help you understand the importance of becoming an expert in your field:

- *Improved problem-solving skills*: As you become more knowledgeable in your area of expertise, you'll be able to solve complex problems more efficiently. This can lead to improved productivity and better results in your work.
- *Increased job satisfaction:* When you're an expert in your field, you're more likely to feel confident and satisfied in your work. This can lead to a sense of fulfillment and a greater sense of purpose in your career.
- *Opportunities for mentorship*: As an expert in your field, you can use your knowledge and experience to mentor others. This can be a rewarding experience and can help you develop leadership skills.
- *Networking*: Becoming an expert can also open doors to valuable connections and networking opportunities. By attending industry events and conferences, you can meet other professionals in your field and build relationships that can lead to future collaborations or job offers.

In conclusion, mastering your craft is a crucial step towards achieving your goals and creating opportunities for yourself. It requires dedication, hard work, and a willingness to learn, but the benefits are well worth the effort.

Becoming an expert in your field is a journey that requires a lot of effort, but it is a journey that is worth taking. Here are some other reasons why you should consider mastering your craft:

Proverbs 22:29 (ESV)
"Do you see a man skillful in his work?
He will stand before kings;
he will not stand before obscure men."

- *Enhances your credibility:* Being an expert in your field makes you more credible in the eyes of your colleagues, clients and stakeholders. Your opinions and recommendations are more likely to be taken seriously, and this can help you to build a reputation as a trusted authority in your field.
- *Increases your earning potential:* As an expert, you are more likely to be in high demand, which can lead to increased earning potential. You may be able to command a higher salary or even start your own business and set your own rates.
- *Keeps you up-to-date:* In order to stay at the top of your game, you need to keep up-to-date with the latest developments in your field. By mastering your craft, you can stay ahead of the curve and ensure that you are always aware of the latest trends and innovations.
- *Provides a sense of purpose:* When you are passionate about your work and committed to mastering your craft, you are more likely to feel a sense of purpose and fulfillment. This can lead to a greater sense of job satisfaction and a more positive attitude towards your work.

Summary:

Becoming an expert in your field requires hard work and dedication, but the rewards are significant. From improved problem-solving skills to increased earning potential, there are many reasons why you should consider mastering your craft.

Colossians 3:23–24 (NIV)
"Whatever you do, work at it with all your heart, as working for the Lord, not for human masters,
since you know that you will receive an inheritance from the Lord as a reward.
It is the Lord Christ you are serving."

Mastering your craft can create opportunities and help achieve goals by improving recognition, credibility, and innovation. It also enhances problem-solving skills, job satisfaction, networking, and mentorship opportunities. Becoming an expert requires dedication, hard work, and a willingness to learn, but the rewards include enhanced credibility, earning potential, up-to-date knowledge, and a sense of purpose.

What are you preparing for? What is your passion?

2 Timothy 2:15 (NIV)
"Do your best to present yourself to God as one approved, a worker who does not need to be ashamed and who correctly handles the word of truth."

Proverbs 18:16 (NKJV)
"A man's gift makes room for him,
And brings him before great men."

Though you may rally in unity with your brother or sister, each of you must stride to your own tempo.

This means that while it's good to work together with others, it's also important to focus on your own goals and move at your own pace. It's easy to get caught up in the excitement of collaboration and teamwork, but it's important to remember that each person has their own unique strengths and weaknesses. By focusing on your own goals and working at your own pace, you can ensure that you are making progress towards the things that matter most to you. Here are a few things to keep in mind as you navigate the balance between collaboration and individual achievement:

- Don't be afraid to set boundaries and communicate your needs to others. It's okay to say no to a project or request if it doesn't align with your personal goals.
- Remember that competition can be healthy and motivating, but it's important to avoid comparing yourself to others in a way that undermines your own progress.
- Take time to reflect on your achievements and celebrate your successes, no matter how small they may seem. This will help you stay focused and motivated as you work towards your goals.

Collaboration is a great way to achieve goals, but it is also important to remember that individual achievement is equally important. Here are a few more things to keep in mind as you strive towards your personal goals while working in a collaborative environment:

Galatians 6:4–5 (NIV)
"Each one should test their own actions. Then they can take pride in themselves alone, without comparing themselves to someone else, for each one should carry their own load."

- Be open to feedback from others, but also trust your own instincts. Remember that your unique perspective and skills are valuable assets to the team.
- If you find yourself struggling with a particular task or project, don't be afraid to ask for help. This can be a valuable learning opportunity and can also help you build stronger relationships with your collaborators.
- Remember that collaboration is a two-way street. Make sure you are contributing to the team in a meaningful way and actively listening to the ideas and perspectives of others.
- Finally, don't forget to take care of yourself. Make time for self-care and relaxation, and don't push yourself too hard. Remember that success is a journey, not a destination, and it's important to enjoy the process along the way.

Working collaboratively towards a common goal can be a rewarding experience as it often results in innovative solutions and a sense of shared accomplishment. However, it's important to remember that individual growth and achievement is equally important. Here are a few more tips that can help you effectively balance personal goals and collaborative work:

Philippians 2:3–4 (NIV)
"Do nothing out of selfish ambition or vain conceit. Rather, in humility value others above yourselves,
not looking to your own interests but each of you to the interests of the others."

- Strive to strike a balance between taking feedback from others and relying on your own instincts. While it is important to be receptive to feedback, it's also important to trust your own unique perspective and skills. Remember that your contributions to the team are valuable and necessary.
- Don't hesitate to ask for help when you need it. Everyone needs support at times, and seeking help can be a valuable learning opportunity that can help you grow both individually and as a team player. Additionally, asking for help can strengthen relationships with your collaborators.
- To be an effective collaborator, you need to listen to the ideas and perspectives of others. Be sure to contribute to the team in a meaningful way, while also giving due consideration to the ideas of others. Remember that collaboration is a two-way street and everyone's contributions are important.
- Finally, it is important to take care of yourself. Make sure to prioritize self-care and relaxation, and avoid pushing yourself too hard. Remember that success is a journey, not a destination, and it's important to enjoy the process along the way.

Summary:

To balance collaboration and individual achievement, it is important to focus on personal goals and move at your own pace while working with others. Setting boundaries and communicating needs, avoiding comparison, celebrating successes, being open to feedback, asking for help, contributing meaningfully, listening to others, and prioritizing self-care are all important tips for effectively balancing individual and collaborative work. Collaboration can result in innovative solutions and shared accomplishment, but it's important to remember that individual growth and achievement are equally important.

You may reason mutually, but the creation of that reasoning is a conglomerate of individual thinking

It's true that mutual reasoning involves the coming together of individual thoughts and ideas. In addition to the benefits mentioned, mutual reasoning can also lead to improved relationships and teamwork. When individuals engage in constructive dialogue and actively listen to each other, it can foster a sense of trust and respect among team members. This can create a positive and supportive work environment where individuals feel comfortable sharing their ideas and perspectives.

Furthermore, mutual reasoning can also help to identify and address potential biases or blind spots. By considering multiple viewpoints, individuals can become more aware of their own assumptions and biases, and work to overcome them. This can lead to more equitable and inclusive decision-making processes.

Overall, mutual reasoning is a valuable tool for individuals and teams seeking to approach problems and topics in a collaborative and thoughtful manner. By embracing diverse perspectives and engaging in constructive dialogue, individuals can achieve better outcomes and build stronger relationships.

The benefits of mutual reasoning are not limited to problem-solving alone. In fact, this approach can also help to improve overall relationships and teamwork within a group. When individuals engage in constructive dialogue and actively listen to each other, it fosters a sense of trust and respect among team members. This in turn creates a positive and supportive work environment where individuals feel comfortable sharing their ideas and perspectives.

In addition, mutual reasoning can help to identify and address potential biases or blind spots. By considering multiple viewpoints, individuals can become more aware of their own assumptions and biases, and work to overcome them. This can lead to more equitable and inclusive decision-making processes, which is essential in today's diverse and complex workplace.

Embracing mutual reasoning as a tool for approaching problems and topics in a collaborative and thoughtful manner can lead to better outcomes and stronger relationships. It allows individuals to be open to diverse perspectives and engage in constructive dialogue, leading to a more productive and positive working environment.

Taking the approach of mutual reasoning doesn't just benefit problem-solving, it can also have a positive impact on relationships and teamwork within a group. By engaging in constructive dialogue and actively listening to each other, members of a team can develop a sense of trust and respect, creating a supportive work environment where everyone feels comfortable sharing their ideas and perspectives. This can lead to better communication and cooperation, resulting in a more cohesive and effective team.

Another advantage of mutual reasoning is that it helps to identify potential biases or blind spots. When people consider a variety of perspectives, they can become more aware of their own assumptions and biases, and work to overcome them. This leads to more equitable and inclusive decision-making processes, which are critical in today's diverse and complex workplace.

James 1:19 (NIV)
"Everyone should be quick to listen, slow to speak and slow to become angry."

Summary:

Embracing mutual reasoning as a tool for approaching problems and topics in a collaborative and thoughtful manner can lead to better outcomes and stronger relationships. It allows individuals to be open to diverse perspectives and engage in constructive dialogue, leading to a more productive and positive working environment.

Mutual reasoning involves the coming together of individual thoughts and ideas, and is a valuable tool for collaborative problem-solving. It can also lead to improved relationships, teamwork, and more equitable decision-making. By engaging in constructive dialogue and considering diverse perspectives, individuals can achieve better outcomes and build stronger relationships, leading to a more productive and positive working environment. Mutual reasoning also helps to identify potential biases or blind spots and promotes equity and inclusivity in decision-making processes.

You may love your fellow human being, but you can neither take breaths for them nor equal the thump of their heart.

While we may have love and empathy for others, ultimately each person is responsible for their own life and experiences. Expanding on this idea, it is important to acknowledge that while we can offer support and guidance to those around us, we cannot control their actions or choices. It is up to each individual to take responsibility for their own life path and make the necessary decisions to achieve their goals. Additionally, it's important to recognize that everyone's journey is unique and we all have our own challenges to overcome. By taking ownership of our own experiences, we can empower ourselves to make positive changes and create the life we want for ourselves. Some ways to take responsibility for our own lives include:

- Setting clear goals and creating a plan to achieve them
- Holding ourselves accountable for our actions and decisions
- Seeking help and support when needed, but ultimately making our own choices
- Learning from our mistakes and using them as opportunities to grow and improve
- Taking care of our physical and mental health to ensure we are in the best possible state to pursue our goals.

Building upon the notion of taking responsibility for our own lives, it is important to acknowledge that while external factors can influence our situation, it is ultimately up to us to take control of our lives. By assuming ownership of our experiences, we can better navigate our path and create the future we desire. Here are some additional ways to assume responsibility and take control of our lives:

- Embrace a growth mindset and view challenges as opportunities to learn and grow
- Surround ourselves with positive influences, such as supportive friends and mentors who can serve as sounding boards and offer constructive feedback
- Practice mindfulness and self-reflection to gain a deeper understanding of our values, beliefs, and goals
- Prioritize self-care activities that help us recharge and maintain a healthy work-life balance
- Be proactive in seeking out new opportunities that align with our goals and aspirations.

Proverbs 16:3 (NIV)
"Commit to the Lord whatever you do, and he will establish your plans."

By adopting these strategies and taking ownership of our lives, we can create a sense of purpose and fulfillment that can lead to a more satisfying and rewarding life. Assuming responsibility for our own lives can sometimes feel overwhelming, but it can also be empowering. By acknowledging that we have control over our experiences, we can take steps towards creating the future we desire. Here are some additional ways to take control of our lives and assume responsibility:

- Set clear goals and create a plan to achieve them. This can help us stay focused and motivated.
- Take action towards our goals, even if it means stepping outside of our comfort zone. This can help us build confidence and develop new skills.
- Hold ourselves accountable for our actions and decisions. This means taking responsibility for both our successes and failures, and using them as learning opportunities.
- Practice gratitude and focus on the positive aspects of our lives. This can help us stay motivated and maintain a positive outlook.

By adopting these strategies and taking ownership of our lives, we can create a sense of purpose and fulfillment that can lead to a more satisfying and rewarding life. Remember, taking control of our lives is a process that requires effort, patience and perseverance, but the rewards are worth it.

Summary:

While we can offer support and guidance to others, each person is responsible for their own life and experiences. To take responsibility for our own lives, we can set clear goals, hold ourselves accountable, seek help when needed, and prioritize self-care. By assuming ownership of our experiences, we can better navigate our path and create the future we desire. This process requires effort, patience, and perseverance, but the rewards are worth it.

DON'T GET CAUGHT IN OTHER PEOPLES STUFF!

Chapter 3

Proverbs 26:17 (NIV)
"Like one who grabs a stray dog by the ears is someone who rushes into a quarrel not their own."

To avoid getting involved in other people's problems or drama. It can be interpreted as advice to maintain emotional boundaries and prioritize one's own well-being. Expanding on this, setting boundaries can be a healthy way to maintain relationships with others while also taking care of oneself. It allows us to communicate our needs and limits in a clear way, and can prevent us from taking on other people's emotional baggage. Additionally, it's important to remember that it's not selfish to prioritize our own well-being. In fact, when we take care of ourselves, we're better equipped to support and help others in the long run. So, while it's important to be there for our loved ones, it's equally important to know when to step back and take care of ourselves.

Building on this idea, it's worth noting that setting boundaries can often be difficult, especially if we've never established them before. It may require us to have difficult conversations with people we care about, but ultimately, it can lead to healthier and more fulfilling relationships. Some additional thoughts to consider when setting boundaries include:

- *Be specific about what you need:* When communicating your boundaries, it's important to be clear and specific about what you're comfortable with and what you're not. This can help avoid confusion or misunderstandings down the line.
- *Practice self-compassion:* It's okay to feel guilty or uncomfortable when setting boundaries, but it's important to remind ourselves that we're doing what's best for our well-being. Remember to practice self-compassion and give yourself permission to prioritize your needs.
- *Be consistent*: Once you've established your boundaries, it's important to stick to them. This can help build trust and respect with others, and reinforce the importance of your own self-care.

Overall, setting boundaries is a crucial part of maintaining healthy relationships and taking care of ourselves. By communicating our needs and limits in a respectful way, we can cultivate deeper connections with those around us while also prioritizing our own well-being.

When setting boundaries, it's important to keep in mind that it's not a one-time thing. It's an ongoing process that requires consistent effort and practice. Here are a few more things to consider:

- *Be prepared for pushback:* When you first start setting boundaries, some people may not be used to it and may push back. It's important to stand firm and reiterate your needs in a respectful manner.
- *Flexibility is key:* While it's important to stick to your boundaries, it's also important to be flexible when necessary. Sometimes situations may arise that require you to adjust your boundaries, and that's okay as long as you're doing it in a way that still prioritizes your well-being.

- *Take note of patterns:* If you find that you're constantly having to set the same boundaries with the same person or people, it may be worth examining the underlying issues in the relationship. Are your needs consistently being ignored or dismissed? It may be time to reassess the relationship and decide if it's truly healthy for you.

Proverbs 4:23 (NIV)
"Above all else, guard your heart, for everything you do flows from it."

Summary:
Setting boundaries is an act of self-care, and it's important to prioritize your own well-being. By doing so, you can create deeper, more fulfilling relationships with those around you. Maintaining emotional boundaries and prioritizing one's well-being is crucial to avoid getting caught up in other people's problems or drama. Setting boundaries can be difficult, but it allows us to communicate our needs and prevent taking on other people's emotional baggage. When setting boundaries, it's important to be specific, practice self-compassion, and be consistent. It's an ongoing process that requires effort and flexibility. It's also important to note patterns and reassess relationships that consistently ignore or dismiss our needs. Prioritizing our well-being through setting boundaries is an act of self-care that cultivates deeper, more fulfilling relationships.

Inside you lies a force which, when appropriately grasped and directed, can lift his/her whole race out of the pothole of mediocrity; poverty, and disappointment, and onto the seashore of destiny

Each person has the potential to make a significant impact on their community and achieve great success if they harness and channel their inner strength and talent towards their goals. The quote is a reminder that we are all capable of achieving greatness if we believe in ourselves and work hard towards our objectives. Harnessing our inner strength and talent can be challenging, but it is essential to realize our full potential. Here are some ways to channel our inner strength and talent towards our goals:

Proverbs 4:23 (NIV)
"Above all else, guard your heart, for everything you do flows from it."

- Set clear and achievable goals.
- Focus on what you want to achieve and take action towards it every day.
- Surround yourself with positive and supportive people who can encourage and motivate you.
- Learn from your failures and use them as opportunities to grow and improve.
- Practice self-care and take care of your mental and physical health.
- Stay committed to your goals, even when faced with obstacles or setbacks.

Remember, success is not just about achieving your goals; it is also about the journey and the person you become along the way. So, embrace your inner strength and talent, and strive to make a positive impact in your community.

It's easy to get caught up in life's challenges and forget that we all have the power within us to achieve greatness. The quote serves as a reminder that with hard work and self-belief, anything is possible. Here are some additional tips to help you stay focused and harness your inner strength:

Philippians 3:13–14 (NLT)
"No, dear brothers and sisters, I have not achieved it, but I focus on this one thing: Forgetting the past and looking forward to what lies ahead,
I press on to reach the end of the race and receive the heavenly prize for which God, through Christ Jesus, is calling us."

- Visualize your success and believe that you can achieve it. Positive thinking can go a long way in helping you reach your goals.
- Take small steps towards your objectives every day. Consistency is key, and even the smallest actions can add up over time.
- Celebrate your successes along the way. Acknowledging your progress can help you stay motivated and focused.
- Don't be afraid to ask for help or support when you need it. Sometimes, having a support system can make all the difference in achieving your goals.
- Remember to take breaks and recharge your batteries. Self-care is crucial to maintaining your mental and physical health.

By following these tips and staying committed to your goals, you'll be able to tap into your inner strength and talent and achieve the success you desire. Remember that the journey is just as important as the destination, so enjoy the process and make a positive impact along the way. It's true that life can be challenging at times, but it's important to remember that we have the power to overcome obstacles and achieve greatness. Here are some additional tips to help you stay focused on your goals:

Proverbs 4:25–27 (NLT)
"Look straight ahead, and fix your eyes on what lies before you. Mark out a straight path for your feet; stay on the safe path. Don't get sidetracked; keep your feet from following evil."

- Surround yourself with positive and supportive people who believe in you and your abilities. Their encouragement and motivation can help you stay on track.
- Identify your strengths and use them to your advantage. Recognizing your unique talents and skills can help you overcome challenges and achieve success.
- Learn from failures and setbacks. Instead of giving up, use these experiences as opportunities to grow and improve.
- Create a plan and set achievable goals. Having a clear roadmap can help you stay on track and measure your progress.
- Stay consistent and persistent. Success isn't always immediate, but if you stay committed and persevere, you will eventually achieve your goals.

Remember that success is a journey, not a destination. Embrace the process and enjoy the ride. And don't forget to celebrate your achievements along the way, no matter how small they may seem. With hard work, determination, and self-belief, you can achieve anything you set your mind to.

Summary:

The quote suggests that everyone has the potential to achieve greatness by harnessing their inner strength and talent. To achieve success, one must set clear and achievable goals, take action consistently, surround themselves with positive and supportive people, learn from failures, practice self-care, and stay committed to their goals. Success is a journey, not a destination, and it's important to enjoy the process and celebrate achievements along the way.

Philippians 3:13–14 (NIV)
"But one thing I do: Forgetting what is behind and straining toward what is ahead,
I press on toward the goal to win the prize for which God has called me heavenward in Christ Jesus."

For no man or woman can turn out to be victorious without inspiring the lives of others; anyone who adds to prosperity must flourish in return

Inspiring and contributing to the success of others is important for achieving personal success and prosperity. It's true that success is not a solo journey, and one way to achieve it is through collaboration with others. Here are a few more thoughts to add to your discussion:

- When we collaborate with others, it allows us to leverage different strengths, skills, and perspectives. By working together, we can achieve more than we could on our own.
- Collaboration can also lead to innovation and creative problem-solving. When we bring together people with different backgrounds and experiences, it can spark new ideas and approaches.
- It's important to note that collaboration doesn't mean sacrificing your own goals or needs. Instead, it's about finding ways to work together that benefit everyone involved.
- Celebrating the success of others can also be a source of inspiration and motivation. When we see others achieve their goals, it can remind us of what's possible and encourage us to keep pushing towards our own aspirations.
- Finally, contributing to the success of others is not only a way to create a positive and fulfilling world, but it can also have a ripple effect. By supporting others in achieving their goals, they may be inspired to pay it forward and help someone else in turn.

Proverbs 11:25 (NIV)
"A generous person will prosper; whoever refreshes others will be refreshed."

Collaboration is indeed a powerful tool that can help us achieve our goals and aspirations. Here are some additional thoughts to consider:

- In addition to leveraging different strengths and skills, collaboration can also help us learn from one another. By working with others, we can gain new knowledge and insights that we may not have discovered on our own.
- When collaborating with others, it's important to establish clear communication and expectations. This can help ensure that everyone is on the same page and working towards a shared goal.
- Collaboration can also help build stronger relationships with others. By working together towards a common goal, we can develop a sense of camaraderie and mutual respect.
- Celebrating the success of others can be a powerful way to build a positive and supportive community. By recognizing and acknowledging the accomplishments of others, we can create a culture of encouragement and inspiration.
- Finally, it's important to remember that collaboration is not always easy. It requires open-mindedness, flexibility, and a willingness to compromise. However, the rewards of collaboration can be well worth the effort, leading to greater success, innovation, and personal growth.

Building on the benefits of collaboration, here are some additional thoughts to consider:

Ecclesiastes 4:9–10 (NIV)
"Two are better than one, because they have a good return for their labor:
If either of them falls down, one can help the other up.
But pity anyone who falls and has no one to help them up."

- Collaboration can help us overcome our limitations and biases. When we work with others, we can tap into their perspectives, experiences, and knowledge, which can help us expand our own thinking and overcome our blind spots. This can lead to more well-rounded solutions and better outcomes.
- Collaboration can also help us stay motivated and accountable. When we work with others, we can set goals together and hold each other accountable for achieving them. This can help us stay focused and committed, even when faced with challenges or setbacks.
- Collaboration can be a powerful way to foster creativity and innovation. By bringing together people with diverse backgrounds and perspectives, we can generate new ideas and approaches that we may not have considered on our own. This can lead to breakthroughs and new opportunities.
- Effective collaboration requires trust and respect. When we collaborate with others, we need to be willing to listen to their ideas, give and receive feedback, and be open to different ways of doing things. This requires a willingness to be vulnerable and to trust in the expertise and good intentions of our collaborators.
- Finally, collaboration can be a source of personal fulfillment and satisfaction. When we work with others towards a shared goal, we can experience a sense of purpose and meaning that can be deeply rewarding.

"Collaboration fosters stronger relationships, fostering camaraderie and mutual respect through shared goals."
"Celebrating others' success builds a positive and supportive community, cultivating a culture of encouragement and inspiration."
"Collaboration, though challenging, offers rewards in the form of greater success, innovation, and personal growth."

Summary:

Success is not a solo journey, and collaboration is a powerful tool to help achieve personal goals. Collaborating with others allows for leveraging different strengths, skills, and perspectives, leading to innovation and creative problem-solving. Celebrating the success of others can be a source of inspiration and motivation. Collaboration can also overcome limitations and biases, foster creativity and innovation, and be a source of personal fulfillment and satisfaction. Trust and respect are key to effective collaboration, which requires a willingness to listen, give and receive feedback, and be open to different ways of doing things.

What is it that you see in you that needs to change?

ETHNIC REPRESSION AND UNFAIRNESS

Chapter 4

Isaiah 10:1-2 (NIV)
"Woe to those who make unjust laws, to those who issue oppressive decrees, to deprive the poor of their rights and withhold justice from the oppressed of my people, making widows their prey and robbing the fatherless."

Proverb 29:14 – If a king judges the poor with fairness, his throne will always be secure

This proverb from the Bible emphasizes the importance of just and fair leadership. It suggests that if a king or ruler treats the poor with fairness and equity, their reign will be stable and secure.

Leadership is an essential aspect of governance, and it is crucial to have just and fair leaders who prioritize the needs of their subjects. The proverb highlights the significance of treating the poor with fairness and equity, which is a fundamental principle of leadership. In today's world, this proverb still holds relevance, and it is essential to have leaders who focus on equality and justice for all. Here are some ways that leaders can apply this principle in their leadership style:

- Prioritize policies that promote equality and justice
- Ensure that all citizens have equal access to resources and opportunities
- Listen to the needs and concerns of marginalized communities and take steps to address them
- Encourage transparency and accountability in governance
- Promote a culture of empathy and compassion towards those in need

By adopting these practices, leaders can create a stable and secure environment for their subjects, just as the proverb suggests. It is the responsibility of every leader to ensure that they govern with fairness and equity and prioritize the needs of their citizens.

In addition to the ways mentioned above that leaders can promote fairness and equity, there are other ways that they can prioritize the needs of their subjects. Here are some additional practices that leaders can adopt:

- Foster a culture of inclusivity by celebrating diversity and promoting tolerance
- Encourage civic participation and empower citizens to take an active role in governance
- Invest in education and healthcare to provide a strong foundation for the development of their citizens
- Promote environmental sustainability to ensure that future generations have access to resources
- Recognize and address systemic inequalities that may be present in society

By incorporating these practices into their leadership style, leaders can ensure that they are creating a fair and just society for all. It is important for leaders to continue to prioritize the needs of their citizens and work towards creating a society where everyone is treated with fairness and equity. Leaders have a significant role to play in promoting fairness and equity in society. In addition to the practices mentioned earlier, here are some other ways that leaders can make a difference:

- Invest in infrastructure and job creation to build a strong economy that benefits everyone
- Provide access to affordable housing to ensure that all citizens have a secure place to call home
- Address issues related to public safety and crime to create a safe and secure environment for all residents
- Promote the protection of human rights, including the rights of marginalized groups
- Encourage innovation and creativity to promote economic growth and development

By prioritizing these practices, leaders can create a society that is fair and just for all citizens. It is important for leaders to remain committed to the needs of their subjects and continue to work towards creating a society that is equitable and inclusive.

Summary:
Proverb 29:14 emphasizes the importance of just and fair leadership. Leaders can apply this principle by prioritizing policies that promote equality and justice, ensuring equal access to resources, listening to marginalized communities, promoting transparency and accountability, and fostering empathy and compassion. In addition, leaders can prioritize inclusivity, civic participation, education and healthcare, environmental sustainability, and address systemic inequalities. By investing in infrastructure, providing access to affordable housing, addressing public safety and crime, protecting human rights, and encouraging innovation, leaders can create a society that is fair and just for all citizens.

When you come upon injustices and social wrongs, you must combat them tooth and nail, but you must not - by any means never drop view of the larger fight to expand as a human being

This quote advises to fight against injustices and social wrongs, but to also remember to continue personal growth as a human being. One possible continuation could be:

- It is common to feel overwhelmed by the injustices and inequalities that exist in our world. However, it is important to remember that we can make a difference by taking small actions every day to support causes that matter to us. Whether it's volunteering at a local charity, signing petitions, or simply speaking up when we witness discrimination or prejudice, each of us can contribute to creating a more just and equitable society.
- At the same time, it's important to take care of ourselves and continue to grow as individuals. This might mean learning new skills, pursuing new interests, or seeking out new experiences. By expanding our horizons and challenging ourselves, we become more resilient and better equipped to face the challenges of the world around us.

- Ultimately, the key is to find a balance between fighting for social justice and working on personal growth. When we can do both, we become more effective agents of change and better equipped to make a positive impact on the world.

Expanding our horizons and challenging ourselves is an important aspect of personal growth. However, it can be difficult to know where to start or what steps to take. Here are a few ideas to get you started:

- Take a class or workshop in a subject that interests you, whether it's cooking, photography, or a new language.
- Travel to a new place, whether it's a nearby city or a foreign country. Experiencing new cultures and ways of life can help broaden your perspective.
- Read books or watch documentaries about topics you are unfamiliar with. This can help you gain a better understanding of different perspectives and issues.
- Seek out new experiences, whether it's trying a new food, attending a cultural festival, or participating in a new hobby.

Personal growth is a lifelong journey, and it's important to continue challenging ourselves and learning new things. Expanding our horizons and challenging ourselves can be a daunting task, but it is essential for personal growth. Here are some more ideas to help you on your journey of self-improvement:

- Volunteer in your community to connect with people from diverse backgrounds and to make a positive impact on society.
- Join a group or club that shares your interests or hobbies. This can be an excellent opportunity to meet new people and learn from their experiences.
- Set goals for yourself, both short-term and long-term. This will give you something to work towards and help you stay motivated.

- Take on new challenges at work or in your personal life. This will help you build confidence and develop new skills.

Summary:

Remember, personal growth is a continuous process, and there is always room for improvement. Embrace new experiences and challenges, and never stop learning. This quote encourages fighting against social injustices while continuing personal growth. Balancing the two is important to become an effective agent of change. To expand as a human being, we can take classes, travel, read, or seek out new experiences. Volunteering, joining groups or clubs, setting goals, and taking on new challenges can also help with personal growth. Remember, personal growth is a lifelong journey with room for improvement.

Have you ever been a victim? Explain how you felt and how you came over it?

Romans 5:3–4 (NIV)
"Not only so, but we also glory in our sufferings, because we know that suffering produces perseverance; perseverance, character; and character, hope."

EXCELLENCE

Chapter 5

Colossians 3:23 (NIV)
"Whatever you do, work at it with all your heart, as working for the Lord, not for human masters."

Philippians 4:8 – Finally, brothers, whatever is true, whatever is honorable, whatever is just, whatever is pure, whatever is lovely, whatever is commendable if there is any excellence, if there is anything worthy of praise, think about these things

This verse from Philippians 4:8 encourages us to think about things that are true, honorable, just, pure, lovely, and commendable. It reminds us to focus our thoughts on things that are excellent and worthy of praise.

In a world where negativity and bad news seem to dominate the headlines, it can be easy to get lost in a cycle of pessimism and despair. However, Philippians 4:8 offers a refreshing perspective on how we can choose to direct our thoughts. By intentionally focusing on things that are true, honorable, just, pure, lovely, and commendable, we can cultivate a more positive and hopeful outlook on life. This can have a profound impact on our mental and emotional well-being, as well as on the way we interact with others. So, the next time you find yourself feeling overwhelmed by negativity, take a moment to reflect on Philippians 4:8 and consider how you can apply its wisdom to your own life.

It's no secret that the world can be a tough and challenging place. It's easy to get bogged down by the negativity and bad news that seem to dominate our daily lives. However, there is a way to break free from this cycle of pessimism and despair. By intentionally choosing to focus on positive things, we can shift our perspective and cultivate a more hopeful outlook on life.

Philippians 4:8 offers a roadmap for how we can do just that. By directing our thoughts towards things that are true, honorable, just, pure, lovely, and commendable, we can train our minds to see the good in the world around us. This doesn't mean we should ignore the difficult realities that exist, but rather that we should actively seek out the positive amidst the negative.

By applying this wisdom to our own lives, we can experience a profound impact on our mental and emotional well-being. We may find ourselves feeling more grateful, compassionate, and kind towards others. We may also find that we are more resilient in the face of challenges, and better equipped to handle whatever life throws our way.

So, the next time you feel overwhelmed by negativity, remember Philippians 4:8 and take a moment to intentionally focus on the positive. It may not change the world overnight, but it can certainly change the way we experience it.

It's important to remember that focusing on the positive isn't just a mindset, it's a practice. Here are some practical tips to help you cultivate a more positive outlook:

- Start each day with gratitude: Take a few moments each morning to reflect on what you're thankful for. This can help set a positive tone for the day ahead.
- Surround yourself with positivity: Seek out uplifting content, whether it's through books, podcasts, or social media accounts. Surrounding yourself with positive messages can help counterbalance the negativity that can be so pervasive in our world.
- Practice mindfulness: Mindfulness is the practice of being present in the moment, without judgment. By focusing on the present moment, we can avoid getting caught up in worries about the future or regrets about the past.

By incorporating these practices into our lives, we can train our minds to focus on the good, even when things are tough. And as we cultivate a more positive outlook, we may find that we're better able to weather the storms of life with grace and resilience.

Summary:

Philippians 4:8 encourages us to focus on positive things that are true, honorable, just, pure, lovely, and commendable. By intentionally choosing to focus on positivity, we can cultivate a more hopeful outlook on life and experience a profound impact on our mental and emotional well-being. Practical tips for cultivating positivity include starting each day with gratitude, surrounding ourselves with positivity, and practicing mindfulness. By training our minds to focus on the good, we can better handle the challenges of life with grace and resilience.

Excellence is not calculated by what a man or woman accomplishes, but by the resistance he or she has to overcome to arrive at their goals

True excellence is not determined by what someone achieves, but rather by the challenges they overcome in order to reach their objectives. The idea of measuring excellence based on the challenges overcome rather than the end result is an important one. Here are some additional thoughts on this topic:

- It is often said that the journey is more important than the destination, and this quote aligns with that sentiment. The obstacles that we face along the way can teach us valuable lessons and help us grow as individuals.
- This perspective can also be applied to teamwork and collaboration. A team that works well together to overcome challenges can be considered excellent, even if their final product is not perfect.
- When we focus solely on the end result, we can miss out on the satisfaction and sense of accomplishment that comes from overcoming obstacles. By valuing the process of growth and learning, we can find more fulfillment in our pursuits.
- Of course, it's important to note that achieving goals is still important. The quote doesn't suggest that success isn't valuable, but rather that success should be evaluated in a more nuanced way.

In line with the idea of measuring excellence based on the challenges overcome, it is worth considering the role that failure plays in this process. Failure is an inevitable part of any journey towards success, and it is often through our failures that we learn the most. By embracing failure as an opportunity to learn and grow, we can approach challenges with a more positive and resilient mindset.

Moreover, measuring excellence based on challenges overcome can also help to promote a more inclusive and diverse approach to success. Traditional measures of success often overlook the obstacles that marginalized individuals and groups face, and fail to recognize their contributions towards overcoming these challenges. By valuing the challenges overcome rather than just the end result, we can create a more equitable and inclusive definition of excellence.

Finally, it's worth noting that the journey towards success is rarely a straight line. Often, we encounter unexpected obstacles and setbacks that force us to reassess our approach and adapt to new circumstances. By measuring excellence based on challenges overcome, we can acknowledge the importance of flexibility, perseverance, and resilience in achieving our goals.

When it comes to measuring excellence, failure is an essential part of the process. Failure teaches us valuable lessons that we can use to overcome challenges and grow. It is crucial to embrace failure as an opportunity to learn and develop a more positive and resilient mindset. By doing so, we can approach challenges with more confidence and creativity.

Moreover, measuring excellence based on the challenges overcome promotes inclusivity and diversity. It acknowledges the obstacles that marginalized individuals and groups face and recognizes their contributions towards overcoming them. This approach creates a more equitable and inclusive definition of excellence, which encourages everyone to strive towards their goals.

It's important to remember that success is seldom a straight line. We often encounter unexpected setbacks and obstacles that force us to reassess our approach and adapt to new circumstances. Measuring excellence based on the challenges overcome acknowledges the importance of flexibility, perseverance, and resilience in achieving our goals. By adopting this approach, we can become more adaptable, resilient, and better equipped to overcome whatever challenges we may face on our journey to success.

Summary:

Excellence is measured by the resistance one overcomes to reach their goals, not just the end result. This perspective values the journey towards growth and learning, rather than just the final outcome. Failure is an essential part of this process, teaching us valuable lessons that help us overcome challenges and grow. Measuring excellence based on challenges overcome promotes inclusivity and diversity, recognizing and valuing the obstacles that marginalized individuals and groups face. It also acknowledges the importance of flexibility, perseverance, and resilience in achieving our goals, as success is seldom a straight line.

Lack of knowledge is no longer a satisfactory excuse for failure because almost all limitations are self imposed

One's own beliefs and mindset can be the biggest obstacles to success, and that gaining knowledge and challenging oneself can lead to overcoming those limitations. Expanding on this idea, here are some possible related points:

James 1:2–4 (NIV)
**"Consider it pure joy, my brothers and sisters, whenever you face trials of many kinds,
because you know that the testing of your faith produces perseverance.
Let perseverance finish its work so that you may be mature and complete, not lacking anything."**

- Our beliefs and mindset are shaped by our experiences, upbringing, culture, and environment, among other factors. They can be limiting or empowering, depending on how we interpret and apply them.
- Sometimes we hold onto beliefs that are no longer valid or helpful, simply because they are familiar or comfortable. We may resist change or new information that challenges those beliefs, even if it could benefit us in the long run.
- To overcome our own limitations, we need to be open-minded, curious, and willing to learn. This requires humility, patience, and a growth mindset that sees failures and setbacks as opportunities to improve and evolve.
- Gaining knowledge and challenging ourselves can take many forms, such as reading books, attending courses, seeking feedback, experimenting with new approaches, or exposing ourselves to diverse perspectives. The key is to find the methods that work best for us and to apply them consistently over time.
- By doing so, we can expand our awareness, skills, and creativity, and realize our full potential. We can also inspire and support others to do the same, creating a positive ripple effect that benefits ourselves and the world around us.
Building off of these points, here are some additional thoughts to consider:
- It's important to recognize that our beliefs and mindset can also be influenced by external factors, such as media, advertising, and societal norms. Being aware of these influences and questioning them can help us develop a more authentic and independent perspective.

Romans 12:2 (NIV)
"Do not conform to the pattern of this world, but be transformed by the renewing of your mind.
Then you will be able to test and approve what God's will is—his good, pleasing and perfect will."

- While it's important to challenge our own limiting beliefs, it's also important to approach this process with self-compassion and understanding. It's okay to have doubts and fears, and it's important to give ourselves time and space to work through them.
- In addition to seeking out new knowledge and experiences, it's also valuable to reflect on our past experiences and how they have shaped us. This can help us better understand ourselves and our patterns of thinking, and identify areas where we may need to make changes.
- It's important to remember that personal growth is a lifelong process, and that there will always be new challenges and opportunities to learn and evolve. By staying open-minded and committed to our growth, we can continue to improve and make meaningful contributions to the world around us.

Continuing on the theme of personal growth, here are a few more points to consider:

- Surrounding ourselves with positive and supportive people can make a big difference in our personal growth journey. Having a strong support system can provide encouragement, accountability, and new perspectives.
- Trying new things and stepping outside of our comfort zone can be scary, but it's often where we experience the most growth. Embracing discomfort and being willing to take risks can lead to new opportunities and personal breakthroughs.
- It's important to remember that personal growth is not a linear process. There will be ups and downs, setbacks and breakthroughs. Embracing the journey and being patient with ourselves can help us stay committed to our growth.
- Finally, it's important to celebrate our successes along the way. Taking time to acknowledge and appreciate our progress can help us stay motivated and inspired to continue growing and evolving.

The Audacity To Believe I Am Free

Summary:
Limitations in achieving success are often self-imposed due to personal beliefs and mindset. Overcoming these limitations requires open-mindedness, humility, and a willingness to learn and challenge oneself. Personal growth involves gaining knowledge, expanding awareness, and adopting a growth mindset. It is important to surround oneself with supportive people, try new things, embrace discomfort, and celebrate successes along the way.

Many go through life without the vaguest idea of their true selves and the meaning of life. There are ingredients, like pieces of a mystery, for the future to be placed by you into one magnificent labor of fine art

It's common for people to not know their true selves or the meaning of life. However, you have the power to create a masterpiece out of the pieces of your future. It's true that many people feel lost or uncertain about their purpose in life. But the good news is that you have the ability to shape your own destiny and find fulfillment. Here are some tips to help you along the way:

- Take time to reflect on your values and goals. What matters most to you? What do you want to achieve in life?
- Set small, achievable goals that align with your values. Celebrate each success, no matter how small.
- Surround yourself with positive and supportive people who encourage you to be your best self.
- Embrace your strengths and weaknesses. Everyone has areas of expertise and areas where they need improvement. Focus on your strengths and find ways to develop your weaker areas.
- Practice gratitude. Take time each day to appreciate the good things in your life, no matter how small.

Life is a journey and it's up to you to create the path that's right for you. Don't be afraid to take risks, make mistakes, and learn from them. You have the power to create a masterpiece out of the pieces of your future. It's important to note that discovering one's true self is a lifelong journey that requires patience and self-reflection. Here are some additional tips that can help you on this journey:

- Be open to new experiences and challenges. Trying new things can help you discover what you're passionate about and what brings you joy.
- Don't compare yourself to others. Everyone's journey is unique, and it's important to focus on your own progress rather than comparing yourself to others.
- Take care of your physical and mental health. Eating well, exercising regularly, and getting enough sleep can improve your overall well-being and give you the energy to pursue your goals.
- Seek out mentors or role models who inspire you. Learning from someone who has already achieved what you want to achieve can be incredibly valuable.
- Don't be afraid to ask for help when you need it. Whether it's from a friend, family member, or professional, seeking help when you're feeling lost or overwhelmed can help you gain clarity and perspective.

The journey towards self-discovery and fulfillment is not always easy, but it's worth it. With dedication and patience, you can create a life that aligns with your values and brings you happiness. In addition to the tips mentioned, there are a few more things to keep in mind when embarking on the journey of self-discovery:

- Practice mindfulness and self-awareness. This involves being present in the moment and paying attention to your thoughts, feelings, and bodily sensations. By doing so, you can gain a deeper understanding of yourself and your inner workings.
- Embrace your strengths and weaknesses. Recognize that everyone has their own unique set of strengths and weaknesses, and it's okay to have areas where you need to improve. By focusing on your strengths and working on your weaknesses, you can build a more well-rounded sense of self.
- Journal or reflect on your experiences. Writing down your thoughts and feelings can help you process them and gain insights into yourself. Try setting aside a few minutes each day to reflect on your experiences and explore your emotions.
- Surround yourself with positive influences. Seek out people who support and encourage you, and distance yourself from those who bring you down. Being around positive influences can help you feel more confident and motivated.
- Remember that self-discovery is a lifelong process. You will continue to learn and grow throughout your life, and it's important to be patient and compassionate with yourself along the way. Embrace the journey and enjoy the process of discovering who you truly are.

Summary:
Discovering one's true self and the meaning of life is a lifelong journey. To help you on this journey, reflect on your values and goals, set achievable goals, surround yourself with positive people, embrace your strengths and weaknesses, and practice gratitude. Also, be open to new experiences, take care of your physical and mental health, seek out mentors, and don't be afraid to ask for help. Additionally, practice mindfulness and self-awareness, journal or reflect on your experiences, surround yourself with positive influences, and remember that self-discovery is a lifelong process.

Excellence can only be accomplished if you remain responsive and teachable

To achieve excellence, it is important to be open to learning and responsive to feedback. Here are some possible continuations for the given content:

- Being open to learning means acknowledging that there is always room for improvement and seeking out opportunities to grow. This can involve taking courses, attending workshops, reading books, or simply being curious and asking questions. By actively seeking out new knowledge and skills, we can expand our horizons and become better at what we do.
- Responding to feedback is an essential part of the learning process, as it allows us to see our blind spots and recognize areas where we need to improve. Feedback can come from various sources, such as peers, mentors, supervisors, or customers. It is important to listen carefully to feedback, ask clarifying questions, and take constructive criticism seriously. By doing so, we can avoid repeating mistakes, fine-tune our skills, and ultimately achieve excellence in our work.
- Achieving excellence is not a one-time event, but rather a continuous journey of learning and growth. It requires a mindset of humility, curiosity, and resilience. We need to be willing to challenge our assumptions, embrace new ideas, and persevere through setbacks. By staying open to learning and responsive to feedback, we can continuously improve ourselves and our work, and make a meaningful impact in our personal and professional lives.

In addition to continuously seeking out opportunities to learn and grow, it is also important to apply what we have learned in our daily lives. This can involve setting specific goals, creating action plans, and holding ourselves accountable for making progress. By actively practicing and applying new knowledge and skills, we can develop mastery and achieve greater levels of success.

Moreover, it's crucial to note that learning and growth do not happen in isolation. Collaborating with others, exchanging ideas, and building relationships can all contribute to our personal and professional development. By seeking out diverse perspectives and experiences, we can broaden our understanding of the world and become more effective communicators and problem-solvers.

Ultimately, embracing a growth mindset and committing to lifelong learning can lead to a fulfilling and meaningful life. It allows us to adapt to changing circumstances, overcome challenges, and make a positive impact on the world around us.

To further enhance our growth and development, we should also be open to feedback and constructive criticism. Feedback can help us identify areas for improvement and provide valuable insights that we may not have considered on our own. It's important to approach feedback from a growth mindset perspective, viewing it as an opportunity to learn and improve rather than as a personal attack.

In addition, seeking out mentors or coaches can also be beneficial. Mentors can offer guidance and support, sharing their own experiences and knowledge to help us navigate challenges and achieve our goals. Coaches can provide us with structure and accountability, helping us stay on track and measure our progress.

Lastly, it's important to recognize that growth and development are ongoing processes. It's not a one-time event, but rather a continuous journey. By embracing this mindset and committing to lifelong learning, we can continue to evolve and thrive, both personally and professionally.

Summary

To achieve excellence, it's essential to remain open to learning and be responsive to feedback. This involves acknowledging room for improvement and seeking out opportunities to grow. We should actively practice and apply new knowledge and skills, set specific goals, and hold ourselves accountable for making progress. Collaborating with others, seeking diverse perspectives, and building relationships can all contribute to our personal and professional development. Lastly, growth and development are ongoing processes, and we should embrace a growth mindset and commit to lifelong learning.

Are you responsive or teachable?

Proverbs 9:9 (NIV)
"Instruct the wise and they will be wiser still;
teach the righteous and they will add to their learning."

INTERNAL AREA: THE ULTIMATE FRONTIER

Chapter 6

Luke 17:21 (NIV)
"Nor will people say, 'Here it is,' or 'There it is,' because the kingdom of God is in your midst."

Matthew 22:42 – saying, "What do you think about the Christ? Whose son is he?" They said to him, "The son of David."

Jesus asks his followers about their thoughts on the Christ, and they respond that he is the son of David. The mention of the Christ in this verse refers to the Messiah, who was prophesied to come from the lineage of David. By acknowledging Jesus as the son of David, his followers were affirming their belief that he was the long-awaited Messiah. This was a significant moment in Jesus' ministry as it solidified his identity as the promised Savior. It also highlights the importance of understanding the historical and cultural context of scripture in order to fully grasp its meaning.

Understanding the historical and cultural context of scripture is crucial in fully comprehending its significance. In the case of the Messiah, the Jewish people had been waiting for centuries for the arrival of a savior who would liberate them from oppression and establish a new kingdom. The lineage of David was particularly important because it was believed that the Messiah would be a descendant of King David.

By acknowledging Jesus as the son of David, his followers were affirming their belief that he was the long-awaited Messiah. This not only solidified Jesus' identity as the promised Savior, but it also gave his followers hope that he would fulfill the prophecies and bring about the long-awaited salvation.

Furthermore, the mention of Jesus as the Messiah also speaks to his divinity. In Jewish tradition, the Messiah was not just a political leader, but also a divine figure who would bring about a new era of peace and righteousness. By proclaiming Jesus as the Messiah, his followers were also acknowledging his divine nature and his role in fulfilling God's plan for salvation.

Overall, this verse is a powerful reminder of the importance of understanding the context and history behind scripture. By doing so, we can gain a deeper appreciation for its meaning and significance, and draw closer to God in the process.

The concept of the Messiah is not limited to Jewish tradition. In fact, the idea of a savior who would liberate people from oppression and establish a new kingdom is present in many cultures and religions around the world. For instance, in Hinduism, there is the concept of Kalki, the tenth and final avatar of the god Vishnu, who will appear on a white horse to restore order to the world.

It is interesting to note how different cultures and religions have their own unique interpretations of the concept of the Messiah, yet they all share a common hope for a better future. This is a testament to the power of faith and the human desire for a brighter tomorrow.

Moreover, the concept of the Messiah is not just limited to religious beliefs. It can also be applied to our personal lives. We all face challenges and struggles in our lives, and we often look for someone or something to save us from our troubles. In a way, we are all searching for our own personal Messiah, someone who can bring us hope and salvation.

In conclusion, the concept of the Messiah is a universal one that transcends boundaries of culture, religion, and personal beliefs. By understanding its historical and cultural context, we can gain a deeper appreciation for its significance and apply its lessons to our own lives.

Summary:

Jesus asks his followers about their thoughts on the Christ, and they respond that he is the son of David, acknowledging him as the long-awaited Messiah. This moment solidified Jesus' identity as the promised Savior and gave his followers hope that he would fulfill the prophecies and bring about salvation. Understanding the historical and cultural context behind the Messiah concept is important to grasp its meaning and significance. This concept is not limited to religious beliefs and can be applied to personal struggles as well. The Messiah is a universal concept that transcends boundaries of culture, religion, and personal beliefs.

YOU ARE A INTELLECTUAL BEING - Thoughts and ideas are in fact existing possessions, thoughts create material outcomes and have a commanding, extended -time result on your life

It is true that thoughts and ideas have a significant impact on our lives and can shape our outcomes. One way in which thoughts and ideas can shape our outcomes is through the concept of the self-fulfilling prophecy. This occurs when our beliefs about ourselves or a situation become reality because we unconsciously create circumstances that confirm those beliefs. For example, if we believe we are not good enough for a job, we may subconsciously sabotage our interview or not put enough effort into the application process. On the other hand, if we believe we are capable and deserving of success, we may be more likely to take risks and pursue opportunities that lead to positive outcomes. Therefore, it is important to be mindful of our thoughts and beliefs, and work towards cultivating a positive and growth-oriented mindset.

One way to cultivate a positive and growth-oriented mindset is by practicing self-affirmations, which are positive statements about ourselves that we repeat regularly. By repeating these affirmations, we are training our brains to focus on our strengths and capabilities, rather than our shortcomings. Additionally, surrounding ourselves with supportive and encouraging people can also help us maintain a positive mindset. These individuals can provide us with constructive feedback and help us see challenges as opportunities for growth. Finally, it is important to remember that setbacks and failures are a natural part of the learning process, and we can use them as opportunities to learn and improve. By adopting a growth-oriented mindset, we can develop resilience and overcome obstacles in our personal and professional lives.

Building a positive and growth-oriented mindset can be challenging, but it is achievable with consistent practice and commitment. Here are some additional tips to complement what you've already mentioned:

- Setting realistic goals and breaking them down into smaller, achievable steps can help us stay motivated and focused on our progress.
- Practicing gratitude regularly can help us appreciate what we have and shift our focus away from negative thoughts or emotions.
- Engaging in activities that bring us joy and fulfillment can also help us maintain a positive mindset and improve our overall well-being.
- Seeking out new experiences and challenges can help us expand our knowledge and skills, and build our confidence in our ability to overcome obstacles.

Building a positive and growth-oriented mindset is a journey, not a destination. It requires consistent effort and a willingness to learn and grow. But with time and practice, it can lead to a more fulfilling and successful life.

Our thoughts and ideas have a significant impact on our lives, shaping our outcomes through the self-fulfilling prophecy. Cultivating a positive and growth-oriented mindset can help us overcome obstacles and develop resilience. This can be achieved through practicing self-affirmations, surrounding ourselves with supportive people, and viewing setbacks as opportunities for growth. Setting realistic goals, practicing gratitude, engaging in fulfilling activities, and seeking out new experiences are additional ways to maintain a positive mindset. It requires consistent effort, but a positive and growth-oriented mindset can lead to a more fulfilling and successful life.

- Intellectual and physical well - being.
- Achievement in your elected area of endeavor.
- A sensation of individual accomplishment.

These are three important components of personal fulfillment: maintaining both intellectual and physical health, excelling in one's chosen field, and experiencing a sense of personal achievement. With the focus on personal fulfillment, it's important to take a closer look at each of these three components and explore how they can contribute to a more fulfilling life.

1. Maintaining intellectual and physical health: This is crucial for overall well-being and can greatly impact one's ability to excel in other areas of life. Whether it's through exercise, a healthy diet, or mental stimulation, taking care of both the body and mind should always be a top priority.
2. Excelling in one's chosen field: Finding a career that aligns with one's passions and interests can lead to a greater sense of fulfillment and purpose. Continuously working to improve skills and knowledge in that field can also bring a sense of accomplishment and satisfaction.

3. Experiencing a sense of personal achievement: This can come in many forms, whether it's completing a challenging project, achieving a personal goal, or simply making progress towards something important. Celebrating these achievements, no matter how small, can boost confidence and motivate continued growth.

By focusing on these three components, individuals can cultivate a more fulfilling life and find greater satisfaction in their personal and professional pursuits.

Summary:

Personal fulfillment consists of three components: maintaining intellectual and physical health, achieving excellence in one's chosen field, and experiencing a sense of personal achievement. Taking care of both the body and mind, finding a career aligned with one's passions and interests, and celebrating personal accomplishments can lead to a more fulfilling life.

How is your thought life?

INTELLECTUAL RULE - The most noteworthy quality of intellectual rule is that it can neither be shaped nor distorted.

The intellectual rule is immutable and cannot be altered or manipulated. Based on this statement, it appears that the concept of intellectual rule is seen as something that is fixed and unchangeable. However, it is important to note that there are differing perspectives on this idea, and it may not be universally accepted as true. Here are a few possible points to consider:

3 John 1:2 (NIV)
**"Dear friend, I pray that you may enjoy good health and that all may go well with you,
even as your soul is getting along well."**

- While it's true that some aspects of intellectual rule may be seen as unalterable, such as fundamental laws of mathematics or logic, other areas of intellectual inquiry are constantly evolving and changing. For example, scientific theories are often revised and refined as new evidence emerges.
- It's also possible that the statement is referring to the idea that intellectual rule is not subject to human manipulation or control. In other words, the laws of the universe or the principles of logic exist independently of our beliefs or desires. This idea has been explored by many philosophers and scientists throughout history.
- Finally, it's worth noting that the concept of intellectual rule may be interpreted in different ways depending on the context. Without more information about the specific context in which the statement was made, it's difficult to say exactly what is meant by it.

The concept of intellectual rule, or the idea that certain truths or principles are unchangeable, is a complex and nuanced topic. While some aspects of intellectual rule may be seen as fixed, such as fundamental laws of logic and mathematics, other areas of intellectual inquiry are constantly evolving and changing based on new evidence and discoveries.

In addition, the statement may be referring to the idea that intellectual rule is not subject to human manipulation or control. This notion suggests that the laws of the universe and principles of logic exist independently of our beliefs or desires, and has been explored by many philosophers and scientists throughout history.

It's important to keep in mind that the interpretation of intellectual rule can vary depending on the context. Without additional information, it's difficult to determine the intended meaning of the statement. Nevertheless, exploring the different perspectives on this concept can help deepen our understanding of the nature of knowledge and truth.

The idea of intellectual rule has been debated and discussed by various scholars throughout history. Here are some additional points to consider:

- Intellectual rule can be seen as a form of authority in the realm of knowledge. It establishes a set of principles that are generally accepted and recognized as true.
- Some argue that intellectual rule can be limiting and hinder progress, as it discourages questioning and experimentation. Others contend that it provides a necessary foundation upon which further knowledge can be built.
- The concept of intellectual rule can also be seen as a reflection of societal values and power structures. Who gets to determine what is considered true or false? How does this influence the dissemination of knowledge?
- It's important to consider the role of evidence and empirical data in intellectual rule. While certain principles may be established as true, they can be challenged or revised based on new information.
- Lastly, the idea of intellectual rule raises questions about the nature of truth and objectivity. Is truth something that exists independently of human interpretation, or is it a construct that is shaped by our experiences and beliefs?

Summary:

The concept of intellectual rule suggests that certain principles and truths are unchangeable, although this idea is nuanced and can be interpreted in different ways. While some areas of intellectual inquiry are constantly evolving, other aspects may be seen as fixed. Intellectual rule can be seen as a form of authority in the realm of knowledge, but it can also be limiting and reflect societal values and power structures. The role of evidence and empirical data is also important in intellectual rule, and it raises questions about the nature of truth and objectivity.

We observe only their outcome. You are where you are in understanding, in relationships, even in monetary conditions, because of what you are in thought

Our current situation is a result of our thoughts and actions, rather than simply luck or chance. Our thoughts and beliefs can influence our understanding, relationships, and financial status. It's true that our thoughts and actions play a significant role in shaping our present circumstances. Here are some additional points to consider:

- Our thoughts and beliefs can also impact our mental and physical health. Negative thoughts, for example, can lead to stress, anxiety, and depression.
- On the flip side, cultivating positive thoughts and beliefs can lead to greater resilience and overall well-being.
- It's important to note that external factors beyond our control can also impact our lives, such as systemic inequalities or natural disasters. However, even in these situations, our mindset and actions can influence how we respond and cope.
- By taking ownership of our thoughts and actions, we can begin to make intentional choices that align with our values and goals, ultimately leading to a more fulfilling life.

In addition to the previous points, here are a few more things to consider regarding the impact of our thoughts and actions:

Colossians 3:23 (NIV)
"Whatever you do, work at it with all your heart, as working for the Lord, not for human masters."
This encourages pursuing excellence in one's chosen field with passion and purpose.

- Our thoughts and actions can also influence the people around us. For example, if we consistently exhibit kindness and empathy towards others, we can create a positive ripple effect that extends beyond ourselves.
- Similarly, if we regularly engage in negative behaviors, such as gossip or criticism, we may unintentionally contribute to a toxic environment that brings others down.
- It's important to acknowledge that changing our thoughts and behaviors can be challenging and may require consistent effort over time. However, by practicing self-awareness and self-reflection, we can identify areas for growth and take steps towards positive change.
- Finally, it's worth remembering that our thoughts and actions don't just impact our current circumstances, but also play a role in shaping our future. By setting intentions and taking intentional steps towards our goals, we can create a life that aligns with our values and brings us joy and fulfillment.

Expanding on the impact of our thoughts and actions, here are some additional points to consider:

- Our thoughts and actions have a powerful impact on our own mental and emotional well-being. When we consistently engage in positive thoughts and behaviors, we can cultivate a sense of inner peace and contentment. On the other hand, if we allow negative thoughts and behaviors to dominate our lives, it can lead to stress, anxiety, and even depression.
- It's important to recognize that our thoughts and actions are interconnected. When we have negative thoughts, it can be difficult to engage in positive behaviors, and vice versa. By focusing on changing one aspect, we can begin to shift the other as well.

- One way to cultivate positive thoughts and actions is through gratitude. By regularly practicing gratitude, we can shift our focus towards the good in our lives and develop a more positive outlook. This can lead to a ripple effect of positivity that extends beyond ourselves and impacts those around us.
- It's also important to be mindful of the impact that our thoughts and actions have on the environment and the world at large. By making conscious choices and taking steps towards sustainability, we can contribute to a healthier planet and a brighter future for generations to come.

Our current situation is a result of our thoughts and actions. Our thoughts and beliefs can impact our mental and physical health, relationships, and financial status. We can take ownership of our thoughts and actions to make intentional choices that align with our values and goals, leading to a more fulfilling life. Our thoughts and actions also impact those around us and the environment. By practicing self-awareness and cultivating positive thoughts and behaviors, we can create a ripple effect of positivity that extends beyond ourselves.

RULE OF TRIGGER AND CONSEQUENCE - Thoughts are triggers and conditions in your life are consequences

Our thoughts can trigger certain conditions or consequences in our lives. It emphasizes the importance of being mindful of our thoughts and how they can affect our experiences.
at the power of our mind and the impact it can have on our overall well-being. Here are some additional points to consider:

- Our thoughts can influence our emotions, behaviors, and actions. If we consistently have negative thoughts, it can lead to feelings of anxiety, depression, and stress.
- The concept of the law of attraction suggests that we can manifest our desires by focusing our thoughts and energy on them. This means that if we truly believe in something and think positively about it, we can attract it into our lives.

- Mindfulness practices, such as meditation and journaling, can help us become more aware of our thoughts and train our minds to focus on the present moment. This can lead to greater clarity, calmness, and overall well-being.
- It's important to remember that our thoughts are not always accurate reflections of reality. Sometimes, they can be distorted by our past experiences, biases, and beliefs. By becoming more aware of our thought patterns, we can challenge and reframe them in a more positive and realistic way.

Expanding on the power of the mind, here are some more insights to ponder:

- The placebo effect is a phenomenon where a person experiences a positive health outcome after receiving a treatment that has no therapeutic effect. This suggests that the power of belief and expectation can have a significant impact on our physical health.
- Visualization is a technique that involves creating mental images of desired outcomes. It can be used to enhance performance in sports, improve confidence in public speaking, and reduce anxiety in stressful situations.
- Gratitude practices, such as writing in a gratitude journal or expressing thanks to others, can shift our focus from negative to positive thoughts. This can lead to increased feelings of happiness, contentment, and overall well-being.
- The language we use when talking to ourselves and others can influence our thoughts and emotions. Using positive affirmations and reframing negative self-talk can help us cultivate a more optimistic and empowering mindset.

By taking the time to understand and harness the power of our thoughts, we can improve our mental and physical health, achieve our goals, and live a more fulfilling life. The power of the mind is a fascinating subject, and there are many other insights that can be explored. Here are a few examples:

- The mind-body connection is a well-documented phenomenon, where our thoughts and emotions can impact our physical health. For instance, chronic stress has been linked to a variety of health problems, including high blood pressure, heart disease, and depression.
- Meditation is a mindfulness practice that can help us calm our minds and reduce stress. Research has shown that regular meditation can lead to changes in the brain that are associated with improved mood, increased focus, and decreased anxiety.
- Creative visualization is a technique that involves using mental imagery to create a positive outcome. For example, if you want to achieve a specific goal, you might visualize yourself already having achieved it. This can help you stay motivated and focused on your desired outcome.
- Mindfulness practices, such as yoga and tai chi, can help us cultivate a greater sense of awareness and presence. This can help us stay centered and focused in the present moment, rather than getting caught up in worries about the past or future.

By exploring these and other insights related to the power of the mind, we can gain a deeper understanding of ourselves and the world around us. We can also develop tools and techniques that can help us live more fulfilling and satisfying lives.

Philippians 4:6–7 (NIV)
"Do not be anxious about anything, but in every situation, by prayer and petition, with thanksgiving, present your requests to God. And the peace of God, which transcends all understanding, will guard your hearts and your minds in Christ Jesus."

Summary

The Rule of Trigger and Consequence highlights how our thoughts can trigger certain conditions or consequences in our lives, emphasizing the importance of being mindful of our thoughts. Our thoughts can influence our emotions, behaviors, and actions, and the power of our mind can impact our overall well-being. Mindfulness practices and gratitude practices can help us cultivate a more positive mindset, and visualization and the language we use with ourselves and others can also influence our thoughts and emotions. Understanding and harnessing the power of our thoughts can improve our mental and physical health, help us achieve our goals, and live a more fulfilling life. The power of the mind encompasses the mind-body connection, meditation, creative visualization, and mindfulness practices like yoga and tai chi, which can help us gain a deeper understanding of ourselves and the world around us.

Proverbs 4:23 (NIV)
"Above all else, guard your heart, for everything you do flows from it."

UTILIZE OR SUFFER DEFEAT

Chapter 7

Matthew 25:29 (NIV)
"For whoever has will be given more, and they will have an abundance. Whoever does not have, even what they have will be taken from them."

UTILIZE OR SUFFER DEFEAT - Like physical effort, thought control is entirely a matter of intelligent practice

Practicing intelligent thought control is crucial for success, just as physical effort is necessary to achieve physical fitness. It encourages individuals to utilize their minds to avoid defeat. This statement emphasizes the importance of mental resilience in achieving success. Here are some additional thoughts on this topic:

- Developing a growth mindset can help individuals overcome challenges and persist through setbacks. This involves viewing failures as opportunities to learn and improve, rather than as signs of inherent inability.
- Cultivating self-awareness can also be helpful in avoiding defeat. By understanding one's own strengths and weaknesses, individuals can play to their strengths and seek support or resources to address areas of weakness.
- In addition to mental resilience, it's important to have a clear sense of purpose or motivation. This can help individuals stay focused and committed, even in the face of obstacles or distractions.
- Finally, it's worth noting that avoiding defeat doesn't necessarily mean always succeeding or never experiencing setbacks. Rather, it's about maintaining a positive and proactive mindset, even when things don't go as planned.

It's important to note that mental resilience is not a fixed trait, but rather a skill that can be developed and strengthened over time. Here are some additional thoughts on how to build mental resilience:

2 Timothy 1:7 (NIV)
"For the Spirit God gave us does not make us timid, but gives us power, love and self-discipline."

- Practicing mindfulness and meditation can help individuals cultivate a sense of calm and groundedness, which can be helpful in managing stress and staying resilient in the face of challenges.
- Connecting with supportive friends, family members, or colleagues can also be helpful in building resilience. Having a strong support system can provide a sense of stability and help individuals feel less isolated when facing difficulties.
- Engaging in physical exercise or other forms of self-care can also be beneficial for mental resilience. Taking care of one's physical health can help individuals feel more energized and focused, which can in turn help them stay resilient in the face of challenges.
- Finally, it's important to remember that mental resilience is not just about individual traits or skills, but also about the context in which individuals operate. Factors such as access to resources, social support, and systemic barriers can all impact an individual's ability to be resilient. As such, building a more resilient society requires addressing these broader contextual factors as well.

Expanding on the context of mental resilience, there are several ways to develop and strengthen this skill. Some additional tips include:

Isaiah 40:31 (NIV)
"But those who hope in the Lord will renew their strength.
They will soar on wings like eagles;
they will run and not grow weary,
they will walk and not be faint."

- Learning to reframe negative thoughts and emotions can help individuals build resilience. Instead of seeing challenges as insurmountable obstacles, reframing them as opportunities for growth and learning can help individuals stay motivated and focused.
- Building a sense of purpose and meaning in life can also be helpful in building resilience. This can involve setting goals and working towards them, finding activities that bring joy and fulfillment, or volunteering and giving back to the community.
- Developing problem-solving skills can also strengthen resilience. Learning to break down complex problems into smaller, manageable tasks and coming up with creative solutions can help individuals feel more in control and confident in their ability to overcome challenges.
- Seeking professional help when needed is also an important part of building resilience. This can involve seeing a therapist or counselor, joining a support group, or seeking medical treatment for mental health conditions.
- Finally, it's important to recognize that building resilience is an ongoing process that requires effort and practice. By taking small steps every day to build mental fortitude, individuals can become more resilient and better equipped to handle life's challenges.

Summary

Developing mental resilience is crucial for success and can be built through practicing mindfulness, self-awareness, and cultivating a strong sense of purpose. Mental resilience is not a fixed trait but can be developed and strengthened over time. Building resilience involves reframing negative thoughts, problem-solving, seeking professional help when needed, and taking small steps every day to build mental fortitude. It is also important to recognize that building resilience is an ongoing process that requires effort and practice.

You must use your courage, purpose and power of choice or it will abandon you and you will find that you have none

This statement suggests that courage, purpose, and the power of choice are important qualities to possess, and that failure to exercise them may result in losing them altogether.
Building on the idea that courage, purpose, and the power of choice are important qualities, it's worth noting that these traits are not always easy to develop or maintain. However, there are certain steps you can take to cultivate and strengthen them:

- Practice taking small risks that push you out of your comfort zone. This can help build your courage muscles and make you more comfortable with uncertainty and challenge.
- Reflect on your values and goals regularly to ensure that you are living with purpose and intention. This can help you stay focused on what matters most and make choices that align with your values.
- Be mindful of your decision-making process and try to make choices that align with your goals and values. This can help you exercise your power of choice and avoid feeling like you are at the mercy of circumstances.

By working to develop these qualities, you can not only become more resilient in the face of challenges but also more fully realize your potential and live a fulfilling life.
To further enhance the development of courage, purpose, and the power of choice, there are other helpful steps that you can take:

- Surround yourself with supportive and encouraging people who uplift and challenge you to grow. Having a strong support network can help you navigate difficult situations and give you the courage to take risks.
- Embrace failure as a learning opportunity. By reframing failure as a chance to learn and grow, you can build resilience and become better equipped to handle adversity.

- Take care of your physical and mental health. Self-care practices such as exercise, meditation, and getting enough sleep can help you build the strength and clarity needed to make purposeful decisions and take risks.

By incorporating these steps into your life, you can continue to develop and strengthen the qualities that will serve you well in both personal and professional contexts. Remember that growth and development are ongoing processes, and with dedication and persistence, you can continue to build upon your strengths and lead a fulfilling life.

In addition to the steps mentioned above, there are other helpful ways to enhance personal growth and development:

- Set achievable goals for yourself. By having a clear idea of what you want to accomplish, you can stay motivated and focused on your path towards personal growth.
- Practice self-reflection. Take time to reflect on your experiences, including successes and failures, and what you can learn from them. This can help you gain self-awareness and insight into your values and beliefs.
- Step outside of your comfort zone. Trying new things and taking on new challenges can help you develop confidence and expand your skills and abilities.
- Seek out learning opportunities. Whether it's through formal education, reading, or attending workshops and seminars, continuing to learn and grow can help you stay engaged and motivated.

Personal growth and development is not a one-time event, but an ongoing journey. By incorporating these additional steps into your life, you can continue to build upon your strengths and become the best version of yourself.

Summary

To maintain courage, purpose, and the power of choice, it is important to take small risks, reflect on values and goals, and make mindful decisions. Surrounding yourself with supportive people, embracing failure as a learning opportunity, and practicing self-care can further enhance personal growth and development. Setting achievable goals, self-reflection, stepping outside of comfort zones, and seeking out learning opportunities can also help in becoming the best version of oneself.

RULE OF CORRESPONDENCE - Your external world is nothing more than a mirror or likeness of your internal world

This phrase means that the way you perceive and experience the world around you is a reflection of your own thoughts, beliefs, and emotions. In other words, your external reality is shaped by your internal reality. The way you see the world is a reflection of your own mindset and attitudes.

It's important to note that this concept is not just limited to individual perception, as collective mindsets and attitudes can shape entire societies and cultures. Here are some additional points to consider:

- This idea is often associated with the law of attraction, which suggests that positive thoughts and beliefs can attract positive outcomes and experiences.
- It's possible to change your internal reality and thus influence your external reality by actively working to shift your mindset and beliefs.
- While external factors can certainly impact our lives, such as socio-economic status, access to resources, and systemic inequalities, our internal reality still plays a significant role in how we perceive and respond to those external factors.

- Practicing mindfulness and self-reflection can help us become more aware of our internal reality and how it is shaping our experiences. By doing so, we can become more intentional about cultivating a mindset and attitude that aligns with our goals and values.

"To maintain courage, purpose, and the power of choice, it is important to take small risks, reflect on values and goals, and make mindful decisions. Surrounding yourself with supportive people, embracing failure as a learning opportunity, and practicing self-care can further enhance personal growth and development."
"Setting achievable goals, self-reflection, stepping outside of comfort zones, and seeking out learning opportunities can also help in becoming the best version of oneself."

Expanding on the concept of how collective mindsets and attitudes can shape societies and cultures, it's worth noting that this can lead to both positive and negative outcomes. For instance:

- A society that values inclusivity and diversity is likely to be more accepting of people from different backgrounds and experiences, leading to a more harmonious and tolerant community.
- Conversely, a society that is built on fear and mistrust of others who are different may become more divided and prone to conflict and discrimination.

It's important to recognize that our internal reality is not fixed and can change over time. By actively working to shift our mindset and beliefs, we can create a more positive and fulfilling external reality. Some practical steps we can take include:

Joshua 1:9 (NIV)
"Have I not commanded you? Be strong and courageous. Do not be afraid; do not be discouraged,
for the Lord your God will be with you wherever you go."

- Challenging negative self-talk and replacing it with more positive and empowering thoughts.
- Surrounding ourselves with people who uplift and support us, rather than those who bring us down.
- Engaging in activities that bring us joy and fulfillment, such as hobbies or volunteer work.
- Seeking out resources and support, such as therapy or coaching, to help us navigate challenging times.

Ultimately, by cultivating a positive internal reality, we can create a more fulfilling and meaningful life for ourselves and positively impact those around us. Our mindset greatly influences our perception of the world and how we interact with others. It is crucial to recognize that our internal reality is not fixed and can change over time, allowing us to create a more positive external reality.

To create a society that values inclusivity and diversity, we can take practical steps such as educating ourselves about different cultures and actively seeking out diverse perspectives. By doing so, we can challenge our own biases and prejudices and become more accepting of people from different backgrounds and experiences. In turn, this can lead to a more harmonious and tolerant community.

On the other hand, a society built on fear and mistrust of others who are different can become more divided and prone to conflict and discrimination. It is important to recognize the harmful effects of such attitudes and actively work to shift our mindset towards inclusivity and tolerance.

In addition to challenging negative self-talk, surrounding ourselves with uplifting people, and engaging in fulfilling activities, seeking out resources and support is also essential. Therapy or coaching can be valuable tools to help us navigate challenging times and cultivate a positive internal reality.

By actively working to shift our mindset and beliefs towards inclusivity and diversity, we not only create a more fulfilling and meaningful life for ourselves, but also positively impact those around us and contribute to a more harmonious and tolerant society.

Summary

Our external world is a reflection of our internal world, meaning our mindset and attitudes shape our perception and experiences. This concept can be applied both individually and collectively. To create a positive external reality, we can actively work to shift our mindset towards inclusivity and diversity. This can be achieved by challenging negative self-talk, surrounding ourselves with uplifting people, engaging in fulfilling activities, and seeking out resources such as therapy or coaching. By doing so, we not only create a better life for ourselves but positively impact those around us and contribute to a more harmonious and tolerant society.

RULE OF SUBSTITUTION - The only way to free yourself of any depressing thought is to substitute another for it

This rule suggests that replacing a negative or depressing thought with a more positive one can help improve one's mental state. One's thoughts and emotions are closely connected, and our mindset can greatly impact our mental health. The practice of replacing negative thoughts with positive ones is a technique often used in cognitive-behavioral therapy. It involves identifying negative thoughts and then consciously replacing them with positive, realistic ones. This technique can help individuals develop a more optimistic outlook on life and cope better with challenges. Additionally, research shows that positive thinking can lead to lower levels of stress and anxiety, improved relationships, and better physical health. While it may take some effort to shift your thinking patterns, making a conscious effort to focus on positive thoughts can have a significant impact on your overall well-being.

Our mindset plays a vital role in shaping our mental health as it influences our thoughts and emotions. Negative thoughts can have an adverse effect on our overall well-being, leading to increased levels of stress and anxiety. However, cognitive-behavioral therapy provides an effective solution to combat negative thoughts. By actively recognizing negative thoughts and replacing them with positive, realistic ones, individuals can develop a more optimistic outlook on life. This technique requires conscious effort and practice, but it can lead to significant improvements in mental health. Research shows that positive thinking can not only lower stress and anxiety levels but also improve relationships and physical health. Therefore, it's essential to cultivate a positive mindset and focus on positive thoughts to enhance our overall well-being.

One way to cultivate a positive mindset is to practice gratitude. By focusing on the good things in our lives and expressing appreciation for them, we can shift our perspective from negative to positive. Here are some tips for practicing gratitude:

- Keep a gratitude journal and write down three things you're grateful for each day.
- Express gratitude to others by sending a thank you note or simply telling them how much you appreciate them.
- Take a moment to appreciate the beauty around you, whether it's a sunset or a flower in bloom.
- Practice mindfulness and focus on the present moment, rather than worrying about the past or future.

By incorporating these practices into our daily lives, we can train our minds to focus on the positive and improve our overall well-being.

Philippians 4:8 (NIV)

"Finally, brothers and sisters, whatever is true, whatever is noble, whatever is right, whatever is pure, whatever is lovely, whatever is admirable—if anything is excellent or praiseworthy—think about such things."

Summary

Shifting from negative to positive thoughts can improve mental health. Cognitive-behavioral therapy involves replacing negative thoughts with positive, realistic ones. Positive thinking can reduce stress, anxiety, and improve relationships and physical health. Practicing gratitude, such as keeping a gratitude journal or expressing appreciation to others, can cultivate a positive mindset. By incorporating such practices into our daily lives, we can train our minds to focus on the positive and enhance our overall well-being.

How do you view your circumstances?

When negative thoughts crawl into your subconscious, without delay begin to substitute them with those that are more optimistic

This is a great advice for managing negative thoughts. By consciously replacing negative thoughts with more positive ones, you can improve your overall outlook and mindset. One helpful technique for replacing negative thoughts with positive ones is called reframing. Reframing involves looking at a situation from a different perspective in order to shift your mindset. Here are some ways to reframe negative thoughts into positive ones:

- Instead of thinking "I'm not good enough," try "I am capable of improving and growing."
- Instead of thinking "This situation is hopeless," try "There are solutions and opportunities for me to explore."
- Instead of thinking "I always fail," try "I have had successes in the past and can learn from my failures."

Romans 12:2 (NIV)
"Do not conform to the pattern of this world, but be transformed by the renewing of your mind.
Then you will be able to test and approve what God's will is—his good, pleasing and perfect will."

By practicing reframing regularly, you can train your mind to automatically think more positively and improve your overall well-being. Reframing is a powerful technique that can help you transform negative thoughts into positive ones. By changing the way you perceive a situation, you can shift your mindset and improve your mood. Here are some additional tips on how to reframe negative thoughts:

- Instead of thinking "I'm not good enough," try "I am worthy and deserving of love and respect."
- Instead of thinking "This situation is hopeless," try "I may face challenges, but I am resilient and resourceful enough to overcome them."
- Instead of thinking "I always fail," try "I am constantly growing and learning, and mistakes are a natural part of that process."

In addition to these specific examples, another way to reframe negative thoughts is to ask yourself questions that challenge the validity of your negative beliefs. For example, if you find yourself thinking "I'm a failure," you might ask, "Is that really true? Have there been times when I have succeeded?" By questioning your negative thoughts, you can gain a more balanced perspective and cultivate a more positive mindset. With consistent practice, reframing can become a natural and automatic part of your thinking patterns, leading to greater happiness and well-being.

Reframing is not always easy, but it is an effective way to transform negative thoughts into positive ones. Here are some additional tips to help you reframe your negative thoughts:

2 Corinthians 10:5 (NIV)
"We demolish arguments and every pretension that sets itself up against the knowledge of God, and we take captive every thought to make it obedient to Christ."

- *Recognize your negative thoughts:* The first step in reframing is to recognize when negative thoughts arise. Once you identify them, you can start to challenge them and find a more positive perspective.
- *Practice gratitude:* A great way to reframe negative thoughts is to focus on what you're grateful for. When you're feeling negative, take a moment to write down a few things you're thankful for. This will help shift your focus to the positive aspects of your life.
- *Surround yourself with positivity:* The people you surround yourself with can have a big impact on your mindset. Surround yourself with people who uplift and support you, and try to avoid those who bring you down.

Remember, reframing takes practice and consistent effort, but the more you do it, the easier it becomes. By changing the way you think, you can transform your life and cultivate a more positive mindset.

"By practicing reframing regularly, you can train your mind to automatically think more positively and improve your overall well-being."

"Reframing is a powerful technique that can help you transform negative thoughts into positive ones, allowing you to change your perception of situations and enhance your mood."

Philippians 4:8 (NIV)

"Finally, brothers and sisters, whatever is true, whatever is noble, whatever is right, whatever is pure, whatever is lovely, whatever is admirable—if anything is excellent or praiseworthy—think about such things."

Summary

One way to apply this philosophy in your life is by practicing mindfulness. Mindfulness is the act of being present and fully engaged in the current moment, without judgment. By being mindful, you can observe your thoughts and emotions without reacting to them immediately. This can help you respond to life's challenges in a more thoughtful and deliberate way, instead of reacting impulsively. Additionally, focusing on your reaction rather than trying to control external circumstances can lead to a greater sense of inner peace and acceptance. Remember, life is unpredictable, but your response to it can be intentional and positive.

RULE OF BELIEF - A lot of times belief enables a person to achieve what others consider unachievable.

Belief can be a powerful motivator that helps individuals reach goals that others may perceive as impossible. Belief is a crucial factor that drives people towards achieving their aspirations, especially when faced with challenging circumstances. Here are some additional points that highlight the importance of belief in motivating individuals:

- Belief helps individuals to stay focused on their objectives, even when faced with obstacles and setbacks. It provides the necessary mental fortitude and resilience to keep pushing forward towards one's goals.
- Belief also enables individuals to tap into their full potential, unlocking hidden strengths and abilities that they may not have realized they possessed. This can lead to breakthroughs and accomplishments that may have seemed unattainable otherwise.
- Furthermore, belief can be contagious, inspiring others to adopt a similar mindset and pursue their own aspirations with renewed vigor. This creates a positive ripple effect that can lead to collective progress and success.

In summary, belief is a powerful force that can help individuals to achieve great things and inspire others to do the same. Belief not only helps individuals to stay motivated but also helps in developing a positive attitude towards life. Here are some more points that emphasize the significance of belief in transforming one's life:

- Belief provides individuals with a sense of purpose and direction in life. When one believes in their abilities, they are more likely to set challenging but achievable goals for themselves, leading to a fulfilling and meaningful life.
- Belief also helps individuals to overcome fear and self-doubt. It provides the necessary confidence to take risks and step out of one's comfort zone, leading to personal growth and development.
- Additionally, belief can help individuals to build strong relationships and networks. When one believes in oneself, they are more likely to attract like-minded individuals who share similar values and aspirations, leading to a support system that can help them achieve their goals.

In conclusion, belief is a powerful tool that can help individuals to transform their lives and achieve their aspirations. It provides the necessary confidence, resilience, and positivity to overcome obstacles and unlock one's full potential.

Belief is a powerful force that can help individuals achieve great things in life. Here are some additional points that highlight the importance of believing in oneself:

Mark 9:23 (NIV)
"'If you can'?" said Jesus. "Everything is possible for one who believes."

- Belief can help individuals to maintain a positive outlook on life, even in the face of challenges and adversity. When one believes in their ability to overcome obstacles, they are more likely to maintain a resilient and optimistic mindset.
- Belief can also be contagious. When one person believes in themselves, they can inspire others to do the same. This can create a ripple effect that leads to positive change and transformation on a larger scale.
- Moreover, belief can help individuals to tap into their creativity and imagination. When one believes in their ability to create, innovate, and problem-solve, they are more likely to come up with new and innovative ideas that can lead to success and fulfillment.

In summary, belief is a key ingredient for personal growth, success, and happiness. By cultivating a strong sense of belief in oneself, individuals can achieve their aspirations and make a positive impact on the world around them.

Summary:

Belief is a powerful motivator that helps individuals achieve their goals, even in challenging circumstances. It provides mental fortitude, unlocks hidden strengths, and can be contagious, inspiring others. Belief is also important for personal growth, providing a sense of purpose, overcoming fear and self-doubt, and building strong relationships. Additionally, belief can maintain positivity, inspire creativity and innovation, and create a ripple effect of positive change. Cultivating belief in oneself is a key ingredient for personal growth, success, and happiness.

Do you believe in yourself?

RULE OF ATTRACTION - People are attracted to others like themselves

The concept of the "rule of attraction" suggests that people often find themselves attracted to individuals who share similar characteristics or qualities with themselves. This idea has been explored in various fields, from psychology to sociology and even in the world of dating. Some additional points to consider on this topic are:

- The rule of attraction can also be seen in friendships and professional relationships, where people tend to gravitate towards others with similar interests or work styles.
- This phenomenon can also have negative effects as people may become too comfortable in their own echo chambers and limit themselves from experiencing new perspectives.
- The rule of attraction can also be influenced by societal factors such as cultural norms and values, as well as external factors such as physical appearance and social status.
- It's important to note that while similarities can initially attract people, it's also important to have a balance of similarities and differences in a relationship to promote growth and understanding.

Expanding on the points already mentioned, the rule of attraction has been studied extensively in the field of neuroscience as well. Studies have shown that the brain releases chemicals such as dopamine and oxytocin when we experience attraction towards someone. This can explain why we may feel a strong pull towards someone who shares our interests or values.

However, as mentioned earlier, this can also lead to the formation of echo chambers where we surround ourselves with people who think and act like us, limiting our exposure to new ideas and perspectives. It's important to step out of our comfort zones and interact with a diverse group of people to broaden our horizons.

Cultural norms and values also play a significant role in the rule of attraction. For instance, in some cultures, arranged marriages are still prevalent, and the decision to choose a partner is based on factors such as social status and family background. In contrast, in Western cultures, individuals have more autonomy in choosing their partners based on personal preferences.

In conclusion, while the rule of attraction can explain why we may be drawn towards certain people, it's important to be mindful of the potential drawbacks and to strive for a balance of similarities and differences in relationships. Additionally, being aware of the societal and cultural factors that influence attraction can help us navigate our relationships more effectively.

When it comes to the rule of attraction, it's interesting to note that our subconscious mind also plays a significant role in this process. Our brain processes information at a subconscious level and sends signals to our conscious mind, which can influence our attraction towards someone. This means that we may be drawn towards someone without even realizing it, based on subtle cues such as body language or tone of voice.

Moreover, research has shown that physical attraction can also influence our perception of someone's personality traits. This is known as the "halo effect" and suggests that we tend to attribute positive qualities to someone who we find physically attractive, even if we don't know them well.

It's important to note that while attraction is a natural human instinct, it's also important to be mindful of how it can impact our relationships and interactions with others. As mentioned earlier, surrounding ourselves with like-minded individuals can limit our exposure to diverse perspectives and ideas, which can hinder personal growth and development. Therefore, it's important to seek out new experiences and engage with people who may challenge our beliefs and broaden our horizons.

Summary:

People are often attracted to individuals who share similar characteristics or qualities with themselves, a concept known as the "rule of attraction". This can be seen in friendships, professional relationships, and dating. However, this phenomenon can have negative effects, as people may limit themselves from experiencing new perspectives. The rule of attraction can be influenced by societal factors such as cultural norms and values, as well as external factors such as physical appearance and social status. It's important to have a balance of similarities and differences in a relationship to promote growth and understanding. The subconscious mind also plays a significant role in the process of attraction. While attraction is a natural human instinct, it's important to be mindful of how it can impact our relationships and interactions with others.

Proverbs 27:17 (NIV)
"As iron sharpens iron, so one person sharpens another."

CATCH THE ATTENTION OF LIKE MINDED PEOPLE

Chapter 8

Proverbs 27:17 (NIV)
"As iron sharpens iron, so one person sharpens another."

Optimistic, life - affirming persons catch the attention that of like - minded people

Positive and hopeful individuals tend to attract others who share their optimistic outlook on life. When you exude positivity and hope, you not only attract like-minded individuals but also create a ripple effect. Your optimism and enthusiasm can inspire those around you and encourage them to adopt a more positive mindset. Additionally, research has shown that a positive outlook on life can have numerous benefits, including improved mental health, greater resilience to stress, and even increased lifespan. So don't underestimate the power of positivity - it not only benefits you but can also have a positive impact on those around you.

It is important to note that positivity is not just about being happy all the time or ignoring the challenges that life brings. It is about acknowledging those challenges and choosing to approach them in a way that focuses on finding solutions and opportunities rather than dwelling on the negative. This approach can lead to increased creativity, as well as improved problem-solving skills.

Furthermore, positivity can also enhance relationships, both personal and professional. When you approach interactions with a positive attitude, you are more likely to connect with others and build meaningful connections. This can lead to increased collaboration, improved teamwork, and a more supportive and uplifting environment.

So the next time you are faced with a difficult situation, remember the power of positivity. Choose to approach it with optimism and hope, and watch as your attitude not only benefits you but also inspires those around you.

Luke 6:45 (NIV)
"A good man brings good things out of the good stored up in his heart, and an evil man brings evil things out of the evil stored up in his heart. For the mouth speaks what the heart is full of."

It is true that positivity is not just about being happy all the time. Sometimes life can be challenging, and it is important to acknowledge that. However, maintaining a positive attitude can help you overcome these challenges and approach them with a problem-solving mindset. This can lead to increased creativity and improved problem-solving skills, which are essential in both personal and professional settings.

In addition, approaching interactions with a positive attitude can enhance relationships. When you have a positive outlook, you are more likely to connect with others and build meaningful connections. This can lead to improved teamwork and collaboration, creating a more supportive and uplifting environment for everyone involved.

"Optimistic, life-affirming individuals naturally draw the attention of like-minded people."
"Positivity and hope tend to attract others who share your optimistic outlook, creating a positive ripple effect and inspiring those around you."

It is important to remember that positivity is not just a personal benefit but can also inspire those around you. Choosing to approach difficult situations with optimism and hope can have a ripple effect, spreading positivity and improving the attitudes of those around you. So, next time you face a challenge, remember to focus on finding solutions and opportunities, and choose to approach it with positivity.

Philippians 4:8-9 (NIV)
"Finally, brothers and sisters, whatever is true, whatever is noble, whatever is right, whatever is pure, whatever is lovely, whatever is admirable—if anything is excellent or praiseworthy—think about such things.
Whatever you have learned or received or heard from me, or seen in me—put it into practice. And the God of peace will be with you."

Summary

Positivity and hope attract like-minded individuals and have numerous benefits, including improved mental health, greater resilience to stress, and increased lifespan. It is about acknowledging challenges and choosing to approach them in a way that focuses on finding solutions and opportunities. Positivity can lead to increased creativity, improved problem-solving skills, and enhanced relationships in personal and professional settings. It not only benefits the individual but also inspires those around them.

Achievement attracts additional success, while disappointment attracts more failure

The power of positive thinking and the self-fulfilling nature of our thoughts and actions. Focusing on achievements can attract more success, while dwelling on disappointment can attract more failure. It's important to maintain a positive mindset and keep striving towards our goals.

Maintaining a positive mindset not only helps to attract success but also has several other benefits. Here are a few points that can help to reinforce the power of positive thinking

- Positive thinking helps to reduce stress and anxiety. When we focus on positive thoughts and outcomes, we tend to worry less and feel more confident about our abilities to handle challenges.
- Positive thinking can improve our relationships. When we approach interactions with positivity, we tend to be more open, understanding, and compassionate. This can lead to stronger and healthier relationships with others.
- Positive thinking can improve our physical health. Studies have shown that people who maintain a positive outlook tend to have lower levels of stress hormones, better immune function, and a lower risk of developing certain health conditions.

By focusing on the positive and taking action towards our goals, we can create a self-fulfilling cycle of success and continue to achieve great things in our lives.

In addition to the benefits mentioned above, maintaining a positive mindset can also lead to increased creativity and productivity. When we focus on positive thoughts, we tend to be more open to new ideas and possibilities, which can help us to come up with innovative solutions to problems. Additionally, a positive mindset can help us to stay motivated and focused, allowing us to be more productive and efficient in our work.

It is important to note that maintaining a positive mindset does not mean ignoring or denying negative emotions or situations. Rather, it means acknowledging and accepting them, but choosing to focus on the positive aspects and potential solutions instead of dwelling on the negative.

By cultivating a positive mindset and taking action towards our goals, we can create a fulfilling and satisfying life for ourselves, filled with success, happiness, and meaningful relationships.

In addition to creativity and productivity, maintaining a positive mindset has other benefits that can positively impact our lives. Here are some additional benefits

- Better physical health: Studies have shown that people who have a positive outlook on life tend to have better physical health. They have lower levels of stress, better immune system function, and lower risk of chronic diseases.
- Improved relationships: When we have a positive mindset, we tend to be more optimistic, friendly, and approachable. This can lead to better communication with others, stronger relationships, and a more supportive social network.
- Increased resilience: A positive mindset can help us to better cope with setbacks and challenges. It can give us the strength and motivation to keep going, even when things get tough.

Maintaining a positive mindset is a practice that requires effort and intentionality. By focusing on the positive, accepting the negative, and taking action towards our goals, we can create a more fulfilling and satisfying life for ourselves.

Summary

Focusing on achievements can attract more success and positive thinking has several benefits, including reduced stress, improved relationships, and better physical health. It can also lead to increased creativity, productivity, and resilience. Cultivating a positive mindset requires effort and intentionality, but can create a fulfilling and satisfying life filled with success, happiness, and meaningful relationships.

RULE OF COMPENSATION - It may take countless years for reward to follow virtue

The rule of compensation suggests that it may take a long time for good deeds to be rewarded, but eventually, they will be.

This rule of compensation is often referred to as the law of cause and effect. The idea is that every action has a consequence, and these consequences may not always be immediate. In fact, sometimes it can take weeks, months, or even years for the effects of our actions to manifest

While it can be frustrating to not see immediate results from our good deeds, it's important to remember that they will be rewarded in due time. This can be a comforting thought during difficult times, as it reminds us that our efforts are not in vain.

In addition, the rule of compensation also suggests that negative actions will eventually be punished. This can serve as a reminder to always act with kindness and integrity, as our actions will ultimately come back to us in one way or another.

Overall, the rule of compensation is a powerful concept that encourages us to be patient and persistent in our pursuit of doing good.

The rule of compensation is not just a philosophical concept, but also a practical tool for personal development. By understanding the principle of cause and effect, we can take responsibility for our actions and make better choices in the future. Here are some ways to apply the rule of compensation to our daily lives:

- Practice gratitude: When we appreciate the good things in our lives, we attract more positivity and abundance. By focusing on the positive, we also become more resilient and better able to cope with challenges.
- Act with intention: Before making a decision, consider the potential consequences of your actions. By acting with intention, we can avoid harmful behaviors and cultivate positive outcomes.
- Cultivate empathy: By putting ourselves in other people's shoes, we can better understand and respond to their needs. This not only strengthens our relationships, but also creates a ripple effect of kindness and compassion in the world.

By incorporating these practices into our lives, we can live in alignment with the rule of compensation and create a more fulfilling and meaningful existence.

In addition to the aforementioned ways of applying the rule of compensation to our daily lives, here are some more practical tips that can help us stay on track and make the most out of this principle:

- *Keep a journal:* Writing down our thoughts and feelings can help us gain clarity and insight into our actions and their consequences. By reflecting on our experiences, we can learn from our mistakes and make better choices in the future.
- *Seek feedback*: Asking for feedback from others can help us gain a different perspective and identify blind spots that we may not be aware of. This can help us make more informed decisions and avoid unintended consequences.
- *Learn from others*: Studying the lives and experiences of successful people can provide valuable insights and inspiration for our own personal development. By learning from the wisdom of others, we can avoid common pitfalls and stay motivated on our own journeys.

By incorporating these practices into our daily routines, we can become more mindful and intentional in our actions, and ultimately create a more fulfilling and purposeful life.

Summary

The rule of compensation suggests that good deeds will eventually be rewarded, even if it takes a long time. This principle also applies to negative actions, which will eventually be punished. To apply this rule to daily life, one can practice gratitude, act with intention, and cultivate empathy. Keeping a journal, seeking feedback, and learning from others can also help us make better choices and create a more meaningful life.

Provide generously, with joyfulness, and have no notion of a return

Giving without expecting anything in return, and doing so with happiness and generosity. Giving without expecting anything in return can be a truly fulfilling experience. It feels good to help others and make a positive impact in their lives. Research has shown that giving to others can actually increase our own happiness and sense of well-being.

Here are some ways to practice giving with happiness and generosity:
- Volunteer your time at a local charity or community organization
- Donate to a cause that is important to you
- Offer to help a friend or family member in need
- Practice random acts of kindness, such as paying for someone's coffee or leaving a positive note for a stranger
- Share your skills or expertise with others who could benefit from them

"Provide generously, with joyfulness, and have no notion of a return."
"Giving without expecting anything in return can be a truly fulfilling experience, increasing our own happiness and well-being."

Remember, giving doesn't have to be a grand gesture. Even small acts of kindness can have a big impact on someone's day. So go ahead and give with a happy and generous heart, and see how it can enrich your own life as well as the lives of others.

Giving without expecting anything in return is a selfless act that brings happiness not only to the receiver but also to the giver. The act of giving can create a ripple effect of positivity and kindness that can spread far beyond the initial act.

If you're wondering how to start practicing giving with happiness and generosity, here are some additional ideas:

- Offer to mentor someone in your field of expertise
- Donate your old clothes or household items to a local shelter or thrift store
- Visit a nursing home or hospital and spend time with the residents/patients
- Show appreciation for the people in your life by writing thank you notes or giving small gifts
- Give compliments freely and sincerely to those around you

Summary

Remember, giving doesn't always have to involve money or material possessions. The most valuable thing you can give is your time and attention. So start small, but don't underestimate the power of your actions. Giving with a happy and generous heart can make a world of difference to someone else and to yourself.

If you give looking for or expecting a return, you are not giving, but investing. Are you giving or investing?

"Alter your thoughts - Alter your existence!" is a powerful statement that emphasizes the importance of taking control of your own thoughts in order to change and improve your life. Our thoughts and beliefs have a profound impact on our actions, emotions, and overall well-being. By gaining control over our thoughts, we can shape our reality and create the life we desire.

Here are some strategies to help you take control of your thoughts and, as a result, your life:

Be mindful: Practice mindfulness meditation to cultivate self-awareness and non-judgmental observation of your thoughts. This will help you recognize unhelpful thought patterns and replace them with healthier alternatives.

Cultivate positive thoughts: Focus on positive affirmations, gratitude, and visualization techniques to shift your mindset towards a more optimistic and constructive outlook. Challenge negative thoughts: Identify and question negative thoughts as they arise. Are they based on facts or assumptions? By critically examining your thoughts, you can learn to replace irrational beliefs with more realistic and helpful perspectives.

Surround yourself with positivity: Your environment and the people around you can significantly influence your thoughts. Choose to engage with positive, supportive people and environments that encourage personal growth and well-being.

Set goals and take action: Establish clear, achievable goals for yourself and work towards them. Taking action and making progress towards your objectives can empower you and reinforce positive thought patterns.

Practice self-compassion: Treat yourself with kindness, understanding, and empathy, even when you make mistakes or face setbacks. Remember that everyone has struggles, and self-compassion can help build resilience and facilitate personal growth.

Seek professional help if needed: If you find it challenging to control your thoughts or if they are causing significant distress, consider speaking with a mental health professional who can provide guidance and support.

By consciously shaping your thoughts, you can change your life for the better. Remember that controlling your mind is an ongoing process, and it's essential to be patient and persistent as you work towards altering your thoughts and your existence.

If you must be lackadaisical with your belongings, let it be in association with material things.

"If you must be lackadaisical with your belongings, let it be in association with material things" suggests that if you have to be careless or negligent with your possessions, it is better to do so with material objects rather than with things of greater importance, such as people, relationships, or personal values.

While it is certainly important to prioritize non-material things in life, it is also important to take care of our material possessions, especially those that are valuable or have sentimental value. Being careless with our belongings can lead to unnecessary expense, inconvenience, and even loss. It can also reflect a lack of responsibility and discipline in our character.

Therefore, it is important to strike a balance between valuing material possessions and recognizing their inherent impermanence, while also prioritizing the people, relationships, and values that truly matter in our lives.

PROSPERITY IS NOT ANYTHING OTHER THAN THOUGHT - A man's weaknesses and strength can be brought about or altered only by himself.

A man's weaknesses and strength can be brought about or altered only by himself" suggests that a person's mindset and attitude are key factors in determining their level of success and well-being, and that individuals have the power to change their own weaknesses and strengths.

There is some truth to this statement, as a person's mindset and attitude can certainly have a significant impact on their life outcomes. Positive thinking and a growth mindset can help individuals overcome obstacles, achieve their goals, and thrive in their personal and professional lives. On the other hand, negative thinking and a fixed mindset can lead to self-doubt, fear, and limited opportunities.

However, it is important to recognize that external factors, such as socioeconomic status, access to resources, and systemic barriers, can also play a role in a person's success and well-being. While an individual's mindset and attitude are important, they are not the only factors that determine their outcomes.

Furthermore, while individuals have some agency over their own strengths and weaknesses, it is not entirely accurate to say that they can be "brought about or altered only by himself/herself". Environmental factors such as upbringing, education, and life experiences can also play a significant role in shaping a person's strengths and weaknesses.

Summary

In conclusion, while mindset and attitude are important factors in determining one's success and well-being, it is important to recognize that external factors also play a role. It is also important to acknowledge that an individual's strengths and weaknesses are influenced by both internal and external factors.

"Strike a balance between valuing material possessions and recognizing their impermanence while prioritizing the people, relationships, and values that truly matter in our lives."
"Prosperity is not anything other than thought - a person's weaknesses and strengths can be influenced and changed by their own mindset and attitude."
"Mindset and attitude are key factors in determining success and well-being, but external factors also play a role."

Never allow another person to dictate your existence. There is no such thing as something for nothing

Absolutely, individual autonomy and self-determination are key aspects of personal development and fulfillment. Everyone should have the right and the ability to shape their own life, make their own decisions, and determine their own path. It's important to listen to others and consider their advice, but ultimately, your choices should be your own.

In relation to the second part of your statement, the concept of "no such thing as something for nothing" suggests that everything comes with a price or requires effort. It's a fundamental principle in many areas of life, from economics to personal relationships. For example, achieving success typically requires hard work, perseverance, and sometimes even sacrifice. In relationships, trust and intimacy are built over time through mutual respect, understanding, and consistent effort.

This principle can be a good guideline for personal growth. It encourages us to appreciate the value of hard work, to understand that our actions have consequences, and to accept responsibility for our decisions. It can also foster resilience, as we learn to navigate challenges and overcome obstacles in our pursuit of our goals.

It sounds like you're exploring the concepts of personal agency and the principle of exchange. Both are incredibly important in life.

First, the statement "Never allow another person to dictate your existence" can be interpreted as an assertion of personal agency and autonomy. Every individual has the right and responsibility to define their own life, make their own choices, and shape their own destiny. This isn't to say that we should completely ignore the input, advice, or influence of others. On the contrary, we can often learn and grow from the experiences and perspectives of others. However, the final decisions about what we do, who we become, and what we value should always ultimately be ours to make.

The second part of your statement, "There is no such thing as something for nothing," appears to be referencing the principle of exchange or the concept that everything has a cost. This can be a financial cost, an opportunity cost, or a cost in terms of time, energy, or effort. Even when something appears to be "free," there's often an indirect cost involved. For example, a "free" app might be paid for by advertising revenue, which means that while you aren't paying money to use the app, you're "paying" by viewing (and potentially being influenced by) ads. Or you might be "paying" by allowing the app to collect and use your data.

Both of these ideas can be powerful guiding principles in life. They remind us to take ownership of our lives and decisions, and to be mindful of the costs and consequences of our choices.

I understand you're expressing a belief that every individual should have autonomy over their own lives and actions, and that there is always a cost or consequence to everything, even if it isn't immediately apparent. This is a significant idea that reflects on personal responsibility, independence, and the understanding of the inherent value of things.

Let's break down these ideas further:

Never allow another person to dictate your existence: This is a call to personal autonomy. Each person should have the freedom to make decisions that influence their own lives, within the bounds of respect for the same freedom in others. This is not to say we should completely disregard the advice or influence of others, but rather to make conscious decisions about who and what we allow to guide our actions and thoughts.

There is no such thing as something for nothing: This reflects the principle that all actions and decisions have consequences, and that nothing in life is truly free. Even if something appears to have no cost, there may be an indirect cost or trade-off that isn't immediately apparent. For example, a "free" product may require you to give up personal information, which is then used for marketing or other purposes. In this sense, understanding this principle can help us make more informed and thoughtful decisions.

These ideas encourage an approach to life that values personal responsibility, informed decision-making, and an awareness of the potential consequences of our actions. This perspective can be empowering, but also requires a commitment to ongoing self-reflection and personal growth.

TRANQUILITY OF THE MIND - FREEDOM FROM ALL NEGATIVE EMOTIONS

Chapter 9

Philippians 4:7 (NIV)
"And the peace of God, which transcends all understanding, will guard your hearts and your minds in Christ Jesus."

TRANQUILITY OF THE MIND - Freedom from all negative emotions, - lack of fear, anger, resentment, hatred, jealousy, and guilt.

Achieving peacefulness of the mind and freedom from negative emotions is a worthy goal that many people strive for. While complete freedom from all negative emotions may be difficult to attain, there are steps you can take to cultivate a more peaceful and balanced state of mind. Here are some suggestions:

Self-awareness: Start by becoming more aware of your own emotions and thought patterns. Observe how certain situations or triggers lead to negative emotions. Mindfulness practices such as meditation can help you develop this self-awareness.

Acceptance: Accept that negative emotions are a natural part of being human. Instead of resisting or suppressing them, try to acknowledge and understand them. By accepting your emotions without judgment, you can create space for them to naturally subside.

Emotional intelligence: Develop your emotional intelligence by enhancing your ability to identify, understand, and manage your emotions. This includes being able to recognize the emotions of others and empathize with them. Emotional intelligence helps you respond to challenging situations with greater composure and empathy.

Thought reframing: Negative emotions often stem from negative thought patterns. Learn to identify negative thoughts and challenge them. Replace negative, self-defeating thoughts with more positive and realistic ones. Cognitive behavioral therapy (CBT) techniques can be helpful in this regard.

Gratitude and positivity: Cultivate gratitude by focusing on the positive aspects of your life. Regularly practice gratitude by expressing appreciation for the things you have and the people in your life. Surround yourself with positive influences and engage in activities that bring you joy and fulfillment.

Self-care: Take care of your physical, mental, and emotional well-being. Get enough sleep, eat nutritious food, exercise regularly, and engage in activities that recharge you. Prioritize self-care practices that help you relax and reduce stress, such as taking walks in nature, practicing yoga, or enjoying hobbies.

Seek support: If negative emotions persist or become overwhelming, it may be helpful to seek support from a mental health professional. They can provide guidance and tools tailored to your specific needs and help you work through deep-seated issues that contribute to negative emotions.

Achieving complete freedom from all negative emotions is a lifelong journey, and it's normal to experience fluctuations in your emotional state. The goal is to develop skills and practices that allow you to navigate and manage negative emotions effectively, fostering a greater sense of tranquility and well-being.

"Tranquility of the mind" refers to a state of inner peace and calmness, where one is free from negative emotions and experiences. It is characterized by the absence of fear, anger, resentment, hatred, jealousy, and guilt. Achieving such a state requires self-awareness, emotional regulation, and a positive mindset. Here are some ideas and practices that can help cultivate tranquility of the mind:

Mindfulness: Practice being fully present in the current moment, observing your thoughts and emotions without judgment. Mindfulness meditation and breathing exercises can help develop this skill.

Self-reflection: Take time to reflect on your emotions and understand their underlying causes. Explore your thoughts and beliefs, and consider whether they serve you positively or negatively.

Emotional awareness: Develop the ability to recognize and understand your emotions as they arise. By acknowledging and accepting your emotions without being overwhelmed by them, you can gain greater control over your reactions

Letting go: Practice letting go of negative emotions and releasing attachments to past experiences or grudges. Forgiveness, both towards others and yourself, can contribute to freeing your mind from resentment and guilt.

Positive mindset: Cultivate a positive and optimistic outlook on life. Focus on gratitude, appreciation, and the things that bring you joy. Surround yourself with supportive and uplifting influences.

Self-care: Take care of your physical, emotional, and mental well-being. Engage in activities that promote relaxation and reduce stress, such as exercise, spending time in nature, practicing hobbies, or engaging in creative pursuits.

Compassion and empathy: Cultivate compassion towards yourself and others. Understand that everyone is facing their own challenges, and try to empathize with their experiences. This can help foster understanding and reduce negative emotions like anger or jealousy.

Seek support: Reach out to trusted friends, family members, or professionals if you need support or guidance on your journey towards tranquility. Sometimes, talking to someone can provide valuable insights and perspective.

Achieving tranquility of the mind is a continual process that requires practice and patience. Embrace the journey and be kind to yourself along the way.

Freedom from negative emotions doesn't mean that one should never experience them, as emotions are a natural part of being human. However, tranquility of the mind involves having a healthy relationship with these emotions and not allowing them to control or overpower one's thoughts and actions.

Here are some key aspects that contribute to the tranquility of the mind and the freedom from negative emotions:

- *Self-awareness:* Developing self-awareness allows individuals to recognize and understand their emotions. By being aware of their thoughts and feelings, individuals can better manage and regulate their emotional responses.

Achieving tranquility of the mind is a complex task that requires continuous effort and personal development. This state is often associated with enlightenment and deep understanding in certain philosophical and spiritual traditions. Here are some methods and perspectives that can help cultivate such tranquility:

- Mindfulness and Meditation: Regular practice of mindfulness can improve your ability to regulate your emotions, enhance awareness of your thoughts and feelings, and help you develop a calm and focused mind. There are various forms of meditation that can be useful, like mindfulness meditation, loving-kindness meditation, and more. Cognitive Behavioral Techniques: Cognitive-behavioral therapy (CBT) techniques can help you recognize and challenge negative thought patterns. You can use these techniques to learn how to manage your emotions better and react more positively to stressful situations.

Philippians 4:6–7 (NIV)
"Do not be anxious about anything, but in every situation, by prayer and petition, with thanksgiving, present your requests to God. And the peace of God, which transcends all understanding, will guard your hearts and your minds in Christ Jesus."

- *Gratitude Practice:* Cultivating an attitude of gratitude can help shift your focus from what's wrong in your life to what's right, leading to more positive emotions.
- *Forgiveness:* Holding onto anger and resentment can cause a lot of emotional turmoil. Learning to forgive, both others and yourself, can be a crucial step towards achieving emotional tranquility.
- *Healthy Lifestyle:* Regular physical exercise, a balanced diet, and sufficient sleep are vital for maintaining mental health. These can help regulate your mood and reduce stress.
- *Social Connections:* Building strong and healthy relationships can provide emotional support and increase feelings of self-worth.
- *Spirituality:* For some, spiritual practices or beliefs can provide a sense of purpose, community, and inner peace. Professional Help: If negative emotions are significantly impacting your life, seeking help from a mental health professional may be beneficial. Therapists and counselors can provide guidance and teach techniques for managing your emotions.

Remember, it's normal to experience negative emotions; they're part of the human experience. The goal isn't to eliminate these emotions entirely but to develop a healthier relationship with them so that they don't dominate your life.

ACCURATE MIND APPROACH - That state of mind is the one and only asset over which you have total and uncontested influence

Absolutely, our mind is indeed a powerful tool that we can control and shape according to our needs and wants. This concept is largely rooted in psychological and self-help theories that emphasize personal control, self-awareness, and mindset management. Some key aspects of an "accurate mind approach" might include:

- *Self-awareness:* This is the ability to recognize and understand your moods, emotions, and drives, as well as their effect on others. It is the first step toward regulating your thoughts and behaviors. Mindfulness: This is the practice of focusing your attention on the present moment, while calmly acknowledging and accepting your feelings, thoughts, and bodily sensations. It helps in stress management, emotional regulation, and overall wellbeing. Positive Thinking: Having a positive mindset can significantly influence the outcomes in your life. This doesn't mean ignoring the negatives, but rather, confronting them in a more constructive and optimistic way.

- *Growth Mindset:* This is the belief that abilities can be developed through dedication and hard work. It encourages learning from failures, embracing challenges, and seeing effort as a path to mastery. Emotional Intelligence: This involves recognizing, understanding, and managing our own emotions and the emotions of others. It is essential for effective communication, empathy, and interpersonal relationships. Cognitive Behavioral Techniques: These techniques help in identifying and changing patterns of thinking or behavior that are behind people's difficulties, thus changing the way they feel.

- *Mental Resilience:* This is the ability to bounce back from adversity, adapt to change, and keep going in the face of hardship. By effectively managing and directing our thoughts, we can influence our behaviors and emotions, leading to positive outcomes in various aspects of our lives such as personal relationships, career, health, and overall happiness. However, it's also important to remember that it's okay to seek professional help when dealing with mental health issues, and having control over our minds doesn't mean we should ignore or bypass professional advice.

The "Accurate Mind Approach" seems to be a philosophical concept or strategy, referring to the idea that your mind is the only asset you have total and complete control over. However, as of my knowledge cutoff in September 2021, the specific term "Accurate Mind Approach" has not been officially recognized or widely used in psychology, philosophy, or any other relevant fields.

The idea, however, does bear similarities to several recognized concepts. For example:

- *Stoicism:* This ancient Greek philosophy teaches that we have control over our perceptions and interpretations of the world, even if we cannot control the events themselves. Our internal reactions and attitudes are the only things we truly have control over, according to the Stoics.
- *Cognitive Behavioral Therapy (CBT):* This psychological treatment method is built on the understanding that our thoughts (cognition) influence our feelings and behaviors. By becoming aware of, and then changing, maladaptive or inaccurate thinking, we can improve our emotional state and behavior.

- *Mindfulness and meditation:* These practices often emphasize the importance of observing our thoughts and emotions without judgment. The goal is to cultivate a state of mind that is more objective, accurate, and mindful of the present moment.

The concept you're referring to appears to emphasize the importance of self-awareness, objectivity, and control over one's thought processes. It's about accurately perceiving reality and managing your thoughts and emotions in a way that is constructive and beneficial. The idea also aligns with the understanding that our perceptions and interpretations of the world around us significantly impact our experiences, well-being, and outcomes in life

Indeed, your mindset is a powerful tool that can significantly influence your life. The "Accurate Mind Approach" isn't a recognized term or theory in psychology or neuroscience, but we can infer from your statement that it refers to a mindset that focuses on accuracy, objectivity, and clarity of thought.

Here are some elements that might characterize an "Accurate Mind Approach":

Indeed, your mindset is a powerful tool that can significantly influence your life. The "Accurate Mind Approach" isn't a recognized term or theory in psychology or neuroscience, but we can infer from your statement that it refers to a mindset that focuses on accuracy, objectivity, and clarity of thought.

Here are some elements that might characterize an "Accurate Mind Approach":

Objectivity: This means being able to see things as they truly are, without biases or preconceptions. It requires self-awareness and the ability to separate your own emotions and desires from the situation at hand.

Critical Thinking: This involves analyzing information objectively and making reasoned judgments. It's about examining facts and evidence before forming an opinion or making a decision.

Mindfulness: This is the practice of staying present and fully engaged with what's happening around you. It's about paying attention to your thoughts and feelings without judging them.

Growth Mindset: This is a term coined by psychologist Carol Dweck. It refers to the belief that your abilities can be developed through hard work, good strategies, and input from others. It contrasts with a fixed mindset, which believes that abilities are static. Emotional Intelligence: This is the ability to understand and manage your own emotions, as well as recognize and influence the emotions of others. Emotional intelligence can improve your decision-making and help you navigate social complexities.

Self-Efficacy: This is the belief in one's ability to succeed in specific situations or accomplish a task. It's about understanding your own skills and abilities and believing in your capacity to use them effectively. Resilience: This is the ability to bounce back from adversity, trauma, tragedy, threats, or significant sources of stress. Resilient individuals don't just cope with difficult situations, they learn and grow from them.

These elements, when cultivated and combined, can lead to a mindset that is highly effective and conducive to personal and professional success. Remember, your mind is a tool that you can shape and refine, and doing so can have a significant impact on your life.

WELLBEING AND GET-UP-AND-GO - Anything that affects the health and vigor of the mind will affect the body

Absolutely. There's a significant body of research that supports the notion that our mental health and physical health are interconnected. Here are several ways that the health and vigor of the mind can affect the body:

Philippians 4:13 (NKJV)
"I can do all things through Christ who strengthens me."

- *Exercise:* Physical activity has been shown to improve mental health by reducing symptoms of depression and anxiety. It releases endorphins (chemicals in the brain that act as natural painkillers and mood elevators), reduces immune system chemicals that can worsen depression, and increases body temperature, which may have calming effects.
- *Nutrition:* What you eat can significantly affect your mental health. For example, deficiencies in certain nutrients (like iron and B vitamins) can lead to symptoms of depression. A diet rich in fruits, vegetables, lean protein, and whole grains can help manage mood and energy levels.

"Growth Mindset: The belief that abilities can be developed through hard work and good strategies, contrasting with a fixed mindset that sees abilities as static."

"Emotional Intelligence: The ability to understand and manage your own emotions and influence the emotions of others, enhancing decision-making and social navigation."

"Self-Efficacy: Belief in your ability to succeed in specific situations, rooted in understanding your skills and capacity to use them effectively."

- *Social Relationships:* Positive relationships and social interaction can have a profound effect on mental health. Lack of social connection or support can lead to depression and increased stress levels, which can contribute to physical health issues.

- *Mindfulness and Meditation:* Practices such as yoga, mindfulness, and meditation have been shown to improve mental wellbeing by reducing stress, improving focus, and promoting a general feeling of wellbeing. They can also have physical benefits, such as lowered blood pressure and improved sleep.

- All these factors show that maintaining mental health is vital for physical health. It underscores the importance of a holistic approach to health and wellbeing that addresses both physical and mental aspects

Absolutely, there's a strong interconnection between the mind and body that influences our overall wellbeing. Mental health has direct implications for physical health, and vice versa. Here are a few areas where this is particularly noticeable:

- *Stress:* Chronic stress can lead to several physical problems like heart disease, high blood pressure, diabetes, and other illnesses. It can also lead to mental health problems such as depression and anxiety.
- *Exercise:* Regular physical activity has been shown to decrease symptoms of depression and anxiety. It stimulates the release of endorphins, also known as "feel-good" hormones, which promote feelings of happiness and euphoria.
- *Sleep:* Good sleep is necessary for both physical and mental health. Lack of sleep can affect your mood, memory, and cognitive function, and it has been linked to several physical health problems, including weakened immunity and increased risk of heart disease.
- Nutrition: What you eat directly affects the function of your brain, thus impacting your mood and energy levels. A healthy diet can reduce the risk of chronic diseases, while a poor diet can lead to health problems such as obesity, heart disease, diabetes, and mental health disorders.
- Mindfulness and meditation: These practices can reduce stress and anxiety, improve focus and memory, and increase overall psychological wellbeing. They've also been linked to physical benefits such as lower blood pressure and improved immune function.

So, indeed, any factors that can impact the health and vigor of the mind can significantly affect the body's health, and investing in comprehensive wellbeing practices can contribute to a healthier, more vibrant life.

Absolutely, the mind and body are intricately connected, and the health of one can have profound effects on the other. This is often described as the mind-body connection. Here are a few examples of how this can work:

- *Stress and Anxiety*: High levels of stress or chronic anxiety can lead to physical symptoms such as headaches, stomach issues, high blood pressure, chest pain, and problems with sleep. Over time, these can lead to more serious health problems like heart disease.
- *Depression:* Depression is not just a mental or emotional state. It can also lead to physical symptoms such as fatigue, insomnia, changes in appetite, and chronic pain.
- *Positive Mental Attitude:* On the other hand, having a positive outlook on life can lead to better physical health. People who maintain a positive attitude are more likely to engage in healthy behaviors such as regular exercise and a balanced diet. They also tend to have stronger immune systems and may even live longer.
- *Meditation*: Practices like mindfulness and meditation can have significant benefits for both mental and physical health. These practices can reduce stress, improve concentration, decrease blood pressure, and improve sleep.

Proverbs 17:22 (NIV)
"A cheerful heart is good medicine, but a crushed spirit dries up the bones."

- Exercise: Regular physical activity is not just good for your body, but it can also have mental health benefits. Exercise can help reduce symptoms of depression and anxiety, improve mood, boost self-esteem, and improve sleep. Diet: Eating a healthy diet can boost your mood and energy levels, improving mental health. Certain foods are known to support brain health, like omega-3 fatty acids found in fatty fish, and antioxidants found in fruits and vegetables.

So, prioritizing your mental well-being is crucial for overall health. Similarly, taking care of your physical health can also help improve your mental state. Remember that it's all connected, and small changes in one area can lead to improvements in the other. This is why a holistic approach to health and well-being is often the most effective.

3 John 1:2 (NKJV)
"Beloved, I pray that you may prosper in all things and be in health, just as your soul prospers."

DEVOTED RELATIONS - DO UNTO OTHER'S

Chapter 10

Luke 6:31 (NIV)
"Do to others as you would have them do to you."

"*Devoted Relations* - Do unto others as you would have them do unto you" seems to be a combination of two important concepts, interpersonal devotion and the Golden Rule.

- *Devoted Relations:* This likely refers to relationships in which each person is committed and dedicated to the other's wellbeing. It might include close friendships, family ties, romantic partnerships, and even professional relationships, wherein there is a significant emotional investment and mutual support. It also implies a level of loyalty, steadfastness, and reliability in the way individuals relate to each other. Devotion in relationships often means putting the other person's needs at par with, or even before, your own.

Do unto others as you would have them do unto you: This is often referred to as the Golden Rule, and it is a fundamental principle that's found in many religions and cultures. The concept is simple yet profound: treat others the way you would like to be treated. This encourages empathy, fairness, and mutual respect. It calls for individuals to put themselves in someone else's shoes before deciding on their actions towards them.

In essence, combining these two ideas seems to imply a philosophy or guideline for maintaining strong, respectful, and caring relationships. In a devoted relationship, treating the other person as you'd like to be treated becomes a natural behavior because of the deep emotional connection and mutual understanding. This combination encourages empathy, kindness, and respect in all interactions, leading to healthier, stronger relationships.

Romans 12:10 (ESV)
"Love one another with brotherly affection. Outdo one another in showing honor."

The phrase you're referring to is commonly known as the "Golden Rule," and it's a basic tenet of moral philosophy that's present in many cultures and religions around the world. It encourages us to treat others as we wish to be treated ourselves. This principle fosters empathy, respect, and mutual understanding, promoting a more harmonious society.

In the context of devoted relationships, whether they are familial, platonic, or romantic, the Golden Rule plays a crucial role in maintaining a healthy, balanced, and respectful dynamic.

Here's how it applies:

- *Communication:* Clearly express your feelings, expectations, and thoughts, and be open to hear and understand those of the other person as you'd want your thoughts and feelings understood.
- *Respect:* Treat each person with dignity, recognizing and appreciating their individuality as you would want your uniqueness recognized and valued.
- *Honesty:* Be honest with your loved ones, as trust, which is built on truthfulness, is fundamental in any devoted relationship.
- Support: Offer emotional support and encouragement during challenging times. Remember, you would want the same when facing your own difficulties.
- Patience and Forgiveness: Everyone makes mistakes. Be patient and forgiving with others as you would want them to be with you.
- Equality: Treat others as equals, ensuring fairness and justice in your actions. Remember, you would not want to be treated as less than equal either

- *Freedom:* Give them the freedom to be themselves, to grow and to change, as you would want the same freedom for yourself. These are some ways the Golden Rule can guide us in creating and nurturing devoted relationships. However, it's essential to note that this principle is not about self-sacrifice. It doesn't mean that you should allow others to treat you poorly because you fear to violate this rule. It's about mutual respect and reciprocity in a balanced way.

Devoted relations" and the Golden Rule, "Do unto others as you would have them do unto you," are inherently linked. This rule, which is prevalent in various religious and ethical texts, embodies the principle of empathy and reciprocity in human relationships.

Devoted relationships can be viewed in many forms such as friendships, familial relations, romantic relationships, and even professional interactions. In all of these, the application of the Golden Rule can significantly strengthen and maintain the relationships.

Here are a few ways this could be implemented:

- *Respect:* Treat the other person with the same level of respect that you would want to be treated with. This includes acknowledging their viewpoints and feelings, and being considerate of their circumstances and backgrounds.
- *Communication:* Aim to communicate clearly and honestly, just as you'd appreciate others being transparent with you. Misunderstandings and assumptions often lead to conflicts, so open communication is key.

- *Forgiveness:* We all make mistakes, so offer forgiveness when others err, just as you would hope they'd forgive you. This is not about allowing yourself to be treated poorly, but rather understanding that we all have weaknesses and occasionally get things wrong. Kindness: Be generous with your kindness and goodwill. Even small acts of kindness can go a long way, and it's often the small things that we appreciate most when they're done for us.

- *Support*: Provide emotional and, where appropriate, practical support for the people in your life. We all experience challenges and having a supportive network can make a significant difference.

- *Trust:* Build trust and be trustworthy. You would not want to be lied to or betrayed, so extend the same honesty and loyalty to others.

By practicing the Golden Rule in your relationships, you cultivate an atmosphere of mutual respect, understanding, and love. This principle helps nurture relationships that are rewarding and lasting, contributing to personal and collective well-being.

You can always judge the quality of your life by the number of loving relationships you have entered into.

While the quality of relationships is undoubtedly an important aspect of life quality, it's not the sole determinant. The perception of life quality varies significantly from person to person, and it can be influenced by a broad spectrum of factors, including health, personal development, financial security, achievement, personal freedom, and more.

While the quality of relationships is undoubtedly an important aspect of life quality, it's not the sole determinant. The perception of life quality varies significantly from person to person, and it can be influenced by a broad spectrum of factors, including health, personal development, financial security, achievement, personal freedom, and more.

Moreover, it's essential to note that the number of relationships doesn't necessarily equate to their quality. One can have many relationships, yet they might be superficial or dysfunctional. Conversely, one can have just a few relationships, but they could be deeply loving, fulfilling, and meaningful.

In the context of loving relationships, depth, authenticity, respect, and mutual growth are often seen as key elements. Some individuals may find tremendous happiness and satisfaction in a single, well-nurtured, loving relationship, while others may enjoy their life quality through multiple relationships.

That being said, the presence of loving relationships in a person's life can certainly contribute to overall life satisfaction, emotional well-being, and a sense of belonging and connection, which are all significant components of life quality. However, it's important to consider that everyone has unique needs and priorities when it comes to assessing their quality of life.

Proverbs 15:16-17 (NIV)
"Better a little with the fear of the Lord than great wealth with turmoil.
Better a small serving of vegetables with love than a fattened calf with hatred."

While the number of loving relationships one has can contribute significantly to personal happiness and a sense of well-being, it's important to remember that the quality of life is a multifaceted concept. This phrase seems to suggest that love and relationships are key indicators of a high-quality life, and while they are important, there are many other aspects to consider.

Quality of life often includes not only emotional well-being, but also physical health, financial stability, personal freedom, a sense of purpose, environmental quality, educational opportunities, and social support. It is subjective and varies greatly among individuals based on their personal values, culture, life experiences, and aspirations.

Furthermore, the quality of relationships matters more than their quantity. For instance, one may have a few deep, meaningful relationships that provide much satisfaction and a sense of connection, which can be more fulfilling than having numerous shallow relationships.

In summary, loving relationships are indeed a critical aspect of one's quality of life, but they should not be the sole determinant. A balanced, holistic approach to evaluating life quality is more likely to yield a comprehensive understanding.

That's a beautiful sentiment, and for many people, relationships and the love they carry in them do serve as significant indicators of life quality. However, it's important to note that everyone's criteria for a "good" life can vary.

3 John 1:2 (NIV)
"Dear friend, I pray that you may enjoy good health and that all may go well with you, even as your soul is getting along well."

For some, the number of loving relationships they have might indeed be a key metric. For others, the depth and quality of a few close relationships might be more important than the quantity. Other people might place more value on personal achievements, creative fulfillment, or service to others. And of course, these categories are not mutually exclusive.

It's also essential to keep in mind that entering into many loving relationships doesn't necessarily mean those relationships are healthy or fulfilling. Quality over quantity often holds true in this area of life, as in many others.

Ultimately, the most important thing is to define what a good quality of life means to you personally, as it's a highly subjective and personal matter

ECONOMIC LIBERTY - You may have all the money you desire - the only requirement is that you must earn it.

Economic liberty, often referred to as economic freedom, is the economic philosophy that emphasizes minimal government intervention and maximizes the role of the free market. It embodies the principle that individuals or businesses have the freedom to produce, trade, and consume any goods and services in a manner they deem appropriate, as long as it doesn't infringe upon the rights of others.

The statement you've provided suggests a belief in a form of economic liberty that emphasizes personal responsibility and autonomy. It suggests that anyone can obtain wealth, so long as they've earned it. This can be through entrepreneurship, labor, or any form of economic activity that is rewarded in the market.

This perspective is often associated with classical liberalism, libertarianism, and laissez-faire economics. Proponents argue that economic liberty can lead to innovation, economic growth, and overall societal prosperity. They believe that when individuals have the freedom to choose where to invest their time and resources, they can find the most efficient and satisfying ways to meet their needs and wants.

Critics, however, worry about the potential for wealth inequality, exploitation, and market failures. They argue that without regulation or some form of government intervention, the free market can lead to monopolies, income inequality, and negative externalities like pollution. Furthermore, critics point out that not everyone starts from the same position in life, which can lead to significant disparities in opportunities to earn wealth.

As with most philosophical and economic ideas, the idea of economic liberty is complex, and its implementation can have varied effects depending on the specific context and systems in place.

Economic liberty, as you've described it, aligns closely with the concept of capitalism and free market economics. In such an economic system, individuals and businesses have the freedom to produce, trade, and consume goods and services in a manner that they choose, without substantial interference from a government or other authoritative entity. The primary driving forces are competition and profit motivation. Let's delve into this a little more:

Proverbs 11:1 (ESV)
"A false balance is an abomination to the Lord, but a just weight is his delight."

- *Self-determination:* This principle is a cornerstone of economic liberty, allowing individuals to choose their career path, set their goals, and decide how they want to achieve those goals. The "requirement to earn it" means that economic success is often directly tied to one's efforts, skills, talents, and innovations.
- *Competition and Innovation:* The freedom to earn as much as one can often incentivizes competition and innovation. Different individuals or businesses compete to provide the best goods or services at the most affordable prices. This competition can lead to innovation, as businesses seek new ways to outperform their competitors.

- *Wealth Disparity:* However, the concept of "earning" can be complicated by systemic factors such as inherited wealth, access to quality education, and other socioeconomic conditions. While this system may create opportunities for wealth accumulation and economic mobility, it can also lead to significant wealth disparity.
- *Regulations:* In practice, nearly all capitalist economies also have regulations in place to protect consumers and maintain market competition. This includes rules against fraud, monopolies, and insider trading, as well as safety and quality regulations. These regulations are intended to ensure fair competition and to protect consumers, but they do represent some limitations on absolute economic liberty.
- *Market Failures:* Even with these regulations, capitalist systems can still experience market failures, such as when goods or services are underproduced or overproduced, or when there are significant external costs not captured in market prices (as with pollution, for example).

While economic liberty provides the freedom for individuals to earn wealth, it doesn't guarantee equal outcomes, and can lead to significant inequalities. The key debate around economic liberty tends to revolve around how to balance the advantages of a free market (efficiency, innovation) with the potential disadvantages (inequality, market failures), and what role government should play in this balancing act.

Economic liberty" is a term often used in discussions about political and economic theory. It refers to the freedom of individuals to engage in voluntary transactions and trade, and the freedom of businesses to operate in a free market economy with minimal government intervention.

The concept you described, where one can have as much money as they desire but must earn it, reflects the principles of economic liberty. In this scenario, an individual's wealth is a direct result of their efforts, skills, creativity, risk-taking, and efficiency. This aligns with the principles of capitalism and free-market economies, where personal initiative and hard work are often rewarded with financial gain.

The notion of economic liberty supports the idea of meritocracy - a system in which rewards are given based on merit (in this case, the ability to earn money). However, it's important to recognize that this system isn't perfect and can lead to economic inequality if not managed properly. Some individuals may have more opportunities to earn money due to their social status, education, or geographic location, while others may face systemic barriers that prevent them from earning money.

Ecclesiastes 7:12 (NIV)
"Wisdom preserves those who have it."

In this light, it is essential to consider the role of institutions and public policies in ensuring fairness and equal opportunity. They may need to address any systemic barriers that prevent individuals from participating fully in the economy, such as lack of access to education, healthcare, or basic infrastructure. This is where concepts like social welfare, progressive taxation, and other forms of social safety nets come into play, to balance out the inequalities that can arise in a purely free market system.

In summary, while economic liberty - the freedom to earn and accumulate wealth - is a central tenet of many economic systems, it should ideally be balanced with measures that ensure equal opportunities for all individuals, regardless of their starting point in life.

The only people who make money are those that work in a mint

What is your objective in life? What do you want your reality to be?

Do you have "The Audacity to Believe that YOU are FREE

Psalm 24:1 (NIV)
"The earth is the Lord's, and everything in it,
the world, and all who live in it;"

The Audacity To Believe I Am Free

Contact Information for Booking and for other Books:

THE AUDACITY TO BELIEVE THAT I AM FREE PT:2

**WHEN THE RAIN STARTS TO COME,
DON'T FORGET TO PLANT THE SEEDS**

The Expansion Mentality: The Colors of Success

Email: BookBruceFord@gmail.com
Instagram: BruceFordSpeaks2 - Direct Message
Facebook: Bruce E. Ford

Online Courses: Udemy.com - Words In Motion Leadership Poetry Program

Website: BruceFordSpeaks2.com

More online courses coming Soon

SCAN ME

Call or Text:
770-240-0089 Press Extension 1
Web: KLEpub.com
Email Services@klepub.com

It's time to start and finish   **YOUR Story!**

KLE Publishing specializes in helping people become authors. In as little as 15 to 90 days, we can help you develop your books and e-books and publish to 39,000 outlets! We also offer audiobook services.

Write, Edit, Format, Publish
We can help from
Start to Finish.

Explore and learn more about published authors affiliated with KLE.

KLEPub.com

www.ingramcontent.com/pod-product-compliance
Lightning Source LLC
Chambersburg PA
CBHW070107080526
44586CB00013B/1211